Special INTRO

It's like getting 2 issu

Subscribe now to **Cooking at Home,**
the new recipe magazine from
Company's Coming, and you'll get:

- more delicious, kitchen-tested recipes
- more reliable, easy-to-follow recipes
- more helpful hints
- more color pictures

Plus *a cooking Q&A with Canada's best-loved cookbook author Jean Paré.*

If you enjoy our cookbooks you'll love our magazine.

No Risk! If you're not completely satisfied with *Cooking at Home,* we'll refund you the entire cost of your subscription.

Grant Lovig, Publisher

DETACH AND MAIL THIS CARD TODAY!
or call toll free 1-888-747-7171 and quote reference CBLPXCH.

SUBSCRIBE AND SAVE 33%

✓YES! Send me one year (6 issues) of *Cooking at Home* for just $19.99 (plus taxes) – I'll save 33% off the $29.94 cover price.

NAME _____
(Please Print)

ADDRESS _____ **CITY** _____

PROV/STATE _____ **POSTAL CODE/ZIP** _____

E-MAIL ADDRESS _____

○ Cheque payable to *Cooking at Home* enclosed.
○ Please bill me.
○ Charge my ○ VISA ○ MasterCard

ACCOUNT # _____ **EXPIRY** _____/_____

CARDHOLDER SIGNATURE _____

YOU SAVE $10.00

PRICES OUTSIDE CANADA IN US FUNDS. PLEASE ALLOW UP TO 8 WEEKS FOR DELIVERY OF FIRST ISSUE.
ANNUAL NEWSTAND PRICE $29.94. INTRODUCTORY PRICE GUARANTEED THROUGH 2004.

CBLPXCH

From the name you trust most in recipes

Cooking at Home
CANADA'S OWN RECIPE MAGAZINE

Enjoy great new recipes delivered right to your door every 2 months!

SPECIAL INTRODUCTORY OFFER!

Complete the order form on the reverse and mail today. Or order on-line at www.companyscoming.com

SUBSCRIBE NOW!

6 RECIPE-PACKED ISSUES!

See over....

SAVE
33% NOW

| CANADA | POSTES |
| POST | CANADA |

Postage paid
if mailed in Canada
Business Reply Mail

Port payé
si posté au Canada
Correspondance-
réponse d'affaires

4650557   01

1000008230-L3P8A7-BR01

Cooking at Home

SUBSCRIBER SERVICES
PO BOX 738 STN MAIN
MARKHAM ON   L3P 9Z9

Asian Cooking

Jean Paré

www.**companys**coming.com
visit our web-site

Front Cover

1. Chicken Yakitori, page 78 (Japan)
2. Spicy Radish Salad, page 112 (Asia)
3. Sushi Stacks, page 23 (Japan)
4. Whirl-A-Gig Sushi, page 24 (Japan)
5. Rosy Ginger Pickle, page 38 (Japan)

Props Courtesy Of:
Artifacts
Pier 1 Imports

Back Cover

1. Great Thai Salad, page 114 (Thailand)
2. Thai Coconut Rice, page 131 (Thailand)
3. Coconut Curry Shrimp, page 87 (Thailand)

Props Courtesy Of:
Artifacts
Pier 1 Imports

First Printing March 2002

Canadian Cataloguing in Publication Data

Paré, Jean
   Asian cooking

(Original Series)
Includes index.
ISBN 1-895455-85-5

   1. Cooking, Asian. I. Title. II. Series: Paré, Jean
Original series.

TX724.5.A1P37 2002   641.6'62   C2001-903080-0

Published by
COMPANY'S COMING PUBLISHING LIMITED
2311 - 96 Street
Edmonton, Alberta, Canada T6N 1G3
Tel: (780) 450-6223   Fax: (780) 450-1857
www.companyscoming.com

Company's Coming is a registered trademark owned by Company's Coming Publishing Limited

Printed in Canada

Cooking Tonight?
Drop by companyscoming.com

companyscoming.com

Who We Are | Browse Cookbooks | Cooking Tonight? | Home

everyday ingredients

feature recipes

feature recipes — Cooking tonight? Check out this month's **feature recipes**—absolutely FREE!

tips and tricks — Looking for some great kitchen helpers? **tips and tricks** is here to save the day!

reader circle — In search of answers to cooking or household questions? Do you have answers you'd like to share? Join the fun with **reader circle**, our on-line question and answer bulletin board. Our **reader circle chat room** connects you with cooks from around the world. Great for swapping recipes too!

cooking links — Other interesting and informative web-sites are just a click away with **cooking links.**

cookbook search — Find cookbooks by title, description or food category using **cookbook search**.

contact us — We want to hear from you—**contact us** lets you offer suggestions for upcoming titles, or share your favorite recipes.

Company's Coming
COOKBOOKS®

everyday recipes trusted by millions

Company's Coming Cookbooks

Original Series

- 150 Delicious Squares
- Casseroles
- Muffins & More
- Salads
- Appetizers
- Desserts
- Soups & Sandwiches
- Cookies
- Vegetables
- Main Courses
- Pasta
- Cakes
- Barbecues

- Pies
- Light Recipes
- Preserves
- Light Casseroles
- Chicken
- Kids Cooking
- Breads
- Meatless Cooking
- Cooking For Two
- Breakfasts & Brunches
- Slow Cooker Recipes
- Pizza
- One Dish Meals

- Starters
- Stir-Fry
- Make-Ahead Meals
- The Potato Book
- Low-Fat Cooking
- Low-Fat Pasta
- Appliance Cooking
- Cook For Kids
- Stews, Chilies & Chowders
- Fondues
- The Beef Book
- Asian Cooking
- The Cheese Book **NEW**
  May 1/02

Greatest Hits Series

- Biscuits, Muffins & Loaves
- Dips, Spreads & Dressings
- Soups & Salads
- Sandwiches & Wraps
- Italian
- Mexican

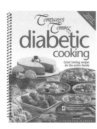

Lifestyle Series

- Grilling
- Diabetic Cooking

Special Occasion Series

- Chocolate Everything
- Gifts from the Kitchen
- Cooking for the Seasons **NEW** *April 1/02*

Table of Contents

The Company's Coming Story 6

Foreword 7

The Flavors of Asia 8

Equipment Guide 10

Garnishes 11

Ingredient Glossary 12

Appetizers 14

Condiments & Spices 33

Desserts & Sweets 42

Main Courses 51

Salads 105

Sauces 117

Side Dishes 122

Soups 140

Measurement Tables 150

Photo Index 151

Tip Index 152

Recipe Index 153

Feature Recipe 157

Mail Order Form 159

Reader Survey 160

The Company's Coming Story

Jean Paré grew up understanding that the combination of family, friends and home cooking is the essence of a good life. From her mother she learned to appreciate good cooking, while her father praised even her earliest attempts. When she left home she took with her many acquired family recipes, a love of cooking and an intriguing desire to read recipe books like novels!

"never share a recipe you wouldn't use yourself"

In 1963, when her four children had all reached school age, Jean volunteered to cater the 50th anniversary of the Vermilion School of Agriculture, now Lakeland College. Working out of her home, Jean prepared a dinner for over 1000 people which launched a flourishing catering operation that continued for over eighteen years. During that time she was provided with countless opportunities to test new ideas with immediate feedback—resulting in empty plates and contented customers! Whether preparing cocktail sandwiches for a house party or serving a hot meal for 1500 people, Jean Paré earned a reputation for good food, courteous service and reasonable prices.

"Why don't you write a cookbook?" Time and again, as requests for her recipes mounted, Jean was asked that question. Jean's response was to team up with her son, Grant Lovig, in the fall of 1980 to form Company's Coming Publishing Limited. April 14, 1981, marked the debut of "150 DELICIOUS SQUARES", the first Company's Coming cookbook in what soon would become Canada's most popular cookbook series.

Jean Paré's operation has grown steadily from the early days of working out of a spare bedroom in her home. Full-time staff includes marketing personnel located in major cities across Canada. Home Office is based in Edmonton, Alberta in a modern building constructed specially for the company.

Today the company distributes throughout Canada and the United States in addition to numerous overseas markets, all under the guidance of Jean's daughter, Gail Lovig. Best-sellers many times over in English, Company's Coming cookbooks have also been published in French and Spanish. Familiar and trusted in home kitchens around the world, Company's Coming cookbooks are offered in a variety of formats, including the original softcover series.

Jean Paré's approach to cooking has always called for quick and easy recipes using everyday ingredients. Even when traveling, she is constantly on the lookout for new ideas to share with her readers. At home, she can usually be found researching and writing  recipes, or working in the company's test kitchen. Jean continues to gain new supporters by adhering to what she calls "the golden rule of cooking": never share a recipe you wouldn't use yourself. It's an approach that works—*millions of times over!*

Foreword

If you crave exotic flavors, vibrant colors and varied textures in your meals, look no further. Asian Cooking has recipes from China, India, Indonesia, Japan, Korea, Malaysia, Philippines, Thailand and Vietnam. I have had the opportunity to visit most of these countries and have friends from all of them. From my travels and conversations with friends, I have learned a great deal about Asian cuisine and culture. Being in the food business, I particularly enjoy the wide variety of food offered in this part of the world.

Throughout Asia, herbs and spices grow in abundance year round, and fish and seafood are caught and sold the same day. Markets are usually within easy walking distance and many people shop daily. The result is refreshing dishes that delight the taste buds. Rice, noodles and fresh fish are staples in most Asian countries, although prepared uniquely in each country. Fresh herbs and spices are also important, along with native fruits and vegetables. In *Asian Cooking*, recipes feature ingredients available in many of our larger grocery stores. Other less common items may be purchased at specialty Asian grocery stores. Check the *Ingredient Glossary*, page 12, to learn more about ingredients specific to Asian cooking.

Stove-top cooking such as stir-frying, steaming, deep-frying and barbecuing are the common methods of food preparation. Check the *Equipment Guide*, page 10, to learn more about special equipment and any suitable substitutes you can use at home. In some of the countries represented in *Asian Cooking*, using a table knife while eating is uncommon since food is prepared in bite-size pieces to accommodate chopsticks, spoons, forks, or eating by hand. To learn the methods and to get acquainted with the foods used in Asian cooking, incorporate one or two recipes into your dinner before venturing into a complete

Asian meal. You may not find some of the ingredients in your kitchen; enjoy the adventure of discovering new ones. In the *Recipe Index*, starting on page 153, look under each country name to find their associated recipes. Make an Asian meal stand out by visiting specialty stores or markets to hunt for inexpensive but beautiful napkins, chopsticks and dishes.

Let *Asian Cooking* bring a world of new tastes to your dining table!

Jean Paré.

Each recipe has been analyzed using the most up-to-date version of the Canadian Nutrient File from Health Canada, which is based upon the United States Department of Agriculture (USDA) Nutrient Data Base.

Margaret Ng, B.Sc. (Hon) M.A.
Registered Dietitian

The Flavors of Asia

China

Chinese food is probably the most familiar of the Asian cuisines in North America. Few items are made ahead of time, except for marinades. Contrast is an important feature in Chinese cooking, whether in color or flavor, so a variety of dishes at one meal is important. Pork is the most widely consumed meat in China. Vegetables are always crisp, though rarely raw and the meat is not overcooked. The meal usually starts with green tea. Dessert is usually fresh fruit.

A Chinese lunch may be rice dumplings stuffed with meat or a bowl of rice or noodles with meat and vegetables. Dinner is more substantial and is made up of several main dishes, not an entrée and side dishes as is the North American custom.

India

As with many warm climates where refrigeration is not widespread, Indian food contains spices originally meant to mask odors but which are now popular in their own right. The best known Indian food is curry, which is a dish that is hot and spicy with a gravy base. Don't confuse it with curry powder, a blend of ten or more spices. There are endless varieties of curry that can be made by using any number of herbs and spices. Cinnamon sticks can be broken up for a subtle flavor. Fresh garlic or gingerroot are more fragrant and have more intense flavor than dried.

Indonesia

Indonesia's 13,000 islands have different culinary specialties, although all residents share a love for the variety of spices which grow abundantly in this equatorial country.

Indian, Chinese, Arab and Dutch traders all left their mark on Indonesian cooking styles. Rice is the most important food crop in this agricultural country and is a part of every meal. Since superb coffee is grown on the island of Java, it is often served with a meal and may be flavored with ginger.

Alternatively, tea or tropical fruit drinks are served while beer or rice liquor is the alcohol of choice. A typical dessert would be steamed, sweetened rice wrapped in fresh leaves or tropical fruit or a sweet pancake concoction.

Japan

Japanese cuisine is all about art form and freshness. It traditionally relies on cooking according to what is in season. Portions are small if they are the freshest ingredients or the first of the season and, therefore, bought at a higher-than-normal price. Garnishes, dishes, taste and layout are equally important in making for an elegant presentation.

Fresh garlic and gingerroot feature highly in Japanese cooking, although using the dried version is acceptable. Ginger may also be pickled and dyed pink to cleanse the palate and please the eye. Heavy spices are not used in Japanese cooking as that would mask the delicate flavors. A Japanese horseradish paste, called wasabi (see *Ingredient Glossary*, page 13), is served to contrast fish. Soy sauce is also common, but Japanese brands are usually lighter in taste, texture and color than Chinese brands. Japanese food is lower in calories than Chinese food, using less cooking oil and lighter sauces. In North America we tend to sprinkle soy sauce on our rice, and although it is a favorite flavor in Japan and China, it is never eaten with rice.

Korea

Korean food has less emphasis on fish and seafood than Japanese cuisine and less cooking oil than Chinese, but more spice than both. Red chili peppers, sesame seeds, green onions and ginger are all common; and pickled vegetables are eaten with nearly every meal. The Korean practice of barbecuing beef has become popular worldwide. Soy sauce, garlic, rice vinegar, sesame oil and dried anchovies flavor various pastes. Noodles are made from rice, buckwheat and mung beans.

Malaysia

Delicate Chinese foods, Indian spices and Southeast Asian herbs combine in Malaysian cuisine along with the influence of Portuguese, Dutch and English cooking. Rice is a staple and is eaten at least once a day. Common spices are cardamom, coriander, cumin, fennel, ginger, shallots and turmeric while herbs, such as lemon grass and kaffir lime leaves (see *Ingredient Glossary*, page 12), are used. Tamarind and lime give tang, while fresh and dried chili peppers give heat to curries. Beef, mutton and seafood are common. Sweet desserts are a must for a Malay meal.

Philippines

Chinese traders and settlers have had a huge impact on this country of 7,000 islands, with many residents now of Chinese-Malay heritage. Along with Chinese rice and noodles, Muslim, Arabs and Indians lent their cumin and coriander. Spaniards introduced garlic, onions, tomatoes, sweet peppers, vinegar, olives and sausage, and the American military left their culinary mark with processed foods, which were readily incorporated. Fish and pork are staples, along with rice which may be made into cakes, noodles or pancakes. Like many other Asian countries, food is laid out all at once rather than in courses, with a variety of condiments, flavorings and dipping sauces to choose from.

Thailand

Thai cooking incorporates the five basic categories of flavors—bitter, hot, salty, sour and sweet—for a taste cornucopia. Color and texture are also varied, so the eyes and taste buds are constantly stimulated. Starting with the staples of rice or noodles and fish, spices are added in different combinations to produce curries unlike the curries of India. Poultry and pork are also principal meats, and chilies are popular—even the seeds and ribs, which are the hottest parts. Spicy soups are best eaten around bites of rice, raw vegetables or fruit to temper the heat. Dessert is either fruit carved into a work of art to resemble another fruit or a sweet dish. Many sweets are not meant to finish a meal in Thailand but rather as a snack since they may be rich and filling.

Herbs and spices commonly used include basil, cardamom, cinnamon, cloves, coriander, cumin, garlic, ginger, lemon grass, lime, mint, tamarind and turmeric. Salt is rarely used in Thai cooking: fish sauce and shrimp paste are used instead. Interestingly, neither leaves a very fishy taste. Instead of using ghee (see *Ingredient Glossary*, page 12) for cooking, coconut oil is used.

Vietnam

Vietnamese food can be described as a combination of Asian and French cooking (due to France's former rule), while keeping its own unique characteristics. Fish and seafood are important in Vietnamese cooking, while beef and pork are also used, and noodles are at least as common as rice. As in other Asian countries, fish sauce is used to add flavor to dishes.

Less cooking oil is used than in French or Chinese cuisine, and there is more simmering and stir-frying than deep-frying. Vietnamese soups have noodles added to differentiate them from a French consommé. The curries aren't as spicy as their Thai or Indian counterparts, but basil, coriander, dill, ginger and mint are used in abundance. Although China is a neighbor, the two cooking styles differ in seasonings, techniques and emphasis on ingredients. For example, shallots and lemon grass (see *Ingredient Glossary*, page 12) are well known in Vietnamese foods but are not used in Chinese food. Fresh or raw vegetables and salads are also popular.

Tea is the most common drink in Vietnam and is served before or after meals, but not during. A family dinner includes soup, rice, a simmered dish and a stir-fried recipe, all served at once. Each person fills a small, wide bowl with rice and places a bit of each main dish (which may be first dipped in a sauce) on the rice. Soup is poured over top. Dessert is usually fresh fruit.

Equipment Guide

Bamboo Steamer Basket: Woven basket that sits above 1 1/2 inches (3.8 cm) of water in a wok or saucepan, elevating food above the water for cooking. Comes in various sizes and is quite inexpensive at Asian specialty stores. The matching lid is often sold separately as they tend to wear out faster than the bottoms because of steam damage. A large saucepan and metal steamer can be used as a substitute.

Chopsticks: Long, thin, round sticks used for eating instead of, or in addition to, cutlery. A fork can be used as a substitute.

Rice Cooker: Electric rice cooker designed to cook rice perfectly. Some models can also be used to steam vegetables and other foods. Follow manufacturer's instructions. Allows for cooking rice in bulk, which can then be frozen in batches for easy reheating. A regular saucepan or pot can be used as a substitute.

Roti Rolling Pin: Very thin version of the rolling pin but slightly larger in the middle than on the ends. Makes rolling out circular dough shapes less of an effort than a regular rolling pin and is used for Indian bread called Roti, page 123. A regular rolling pin can be used as a substitute.

Sushi Mat: Small (approximately 8 × 8 inches, 20 × 20 cm) woven bamboo mat. Used to roll up sushi, a Japanese appetizer, with rice. Waxed paper or parchment paper can be used as a substitute.

Wok: Wide round-bottomed cooking pan used for steaming, stir-frying, stewing, boiling and deep-frying. Provides even heat and is made from rolled steel, aluminum, stainless steel or sheet iron—some with non-stick coating. The round-bottomed version comes with a steel ring to use on a gas stove. Some models have a partially flattened bottom for use on an electric stove. There are also electric models. A frying pan with high sides can be used as a substitute.

Garnishes

Carrot Stars: Cut 1/4 inch (6 mm) thick slices from carrot with diameter of about 1 1/2 inches (3.8 cm). Cut star shape out of slice. Then cut halfway through carrot, from center of star out to an indent (1). Position tip of knife at center, lining up blade with point of star (2). Make next cut diagonally towards the first cut. Remove carrot bit. Repeat all the way around, cutting in the same direction. Pictured on page 126.

Lemon Petal: Cut lemon in half crosswise. Cut 1/8 inch (3 mm) slice from 1 cut end. Cut slice in half. Lay flat on cutting board. Cut between peel and flesh 3/4 of the way around, making sure not to cut peel off. Tuck cut peel towards flesh to resemble cup handle. Pictured on page 89.

Noodle Fan: Break 14 somen noodles into 5 inch (12.5 cm) pieces. Cut piece of nori 1/2 x 2 inches (1.2 x 5 cm). Wrap nori around middle of noodles. Moisten with water to secure. Let stand for 2 minutes until dry. Cut bundle in half through nori. Deep-fry in hot 375°F (190°C) cooking oil in large wok or deep-fryer for about 1 minute until golden and noodles fan out. Drain. Pictured on page 125.

Pepper Triangle: Cut piece off red pepper, removing seeds and ribs. Cut into 2/3 x 1 inch (1.8 x 2.5 cm) rectangles. Cut 1/4 inch (6 mm) slice 3/4 of the way down long side. Turn pepper around. Cut 1/4 inch (6 mm) slice 3/4 of the way down other long side (1). Holding two open ends of pepper, twist into each other to form triangle (2). Pictured on page 90.

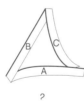

Strawberry Fan: Using whole, firm strawberry, make 4 or 5 parallel cuts from bottom (pointed end) of strawberry towards hull, being careful not to cut all the way through. Gently spread slices apart. Pictured on page 35.

Ingredient Glossary

Bean Threads: Also called cellophane noodles, glass noodles and bean thread vermicelli. Thin, translucent noodles made from green mung bean starch. They need only to be soaked briefly in hot water before use. Found in Asian section of grocery stores.

Bok Choy (bahk-CHOY): Looks like large bunch of leafy celery, with wider white stalks and large curly dark green leaves. Used raw in salads or cooked in stir-fries. Similar, though not the same as Chinese cabbage (see Suey Choy).

Chinese Straw Mushrooms: Delicate-flavored small mushrooms (1 to 1 1/2 inches, 2.5 to 3.8 cm, in diameter) grown on beds of straw. Also called paddy straw mushrooms or grass mushrooms. Found in Asian grocery stores. Small fresh white mushrooms can be used as a substitute.

Curry Paste: A mixture of curry powder, ghee, vinegar and other seasonings. Used as a substitute for curry powder. Thai red curry paste and Indian curry paste can be substituted but there is a subtle difference in flavor. Found in Asian section of grocery stores.

Dashi (DA-shee): Soup stock base made from dried bonito fish flakes and konbu. Used in Japanese cooking and found in Asian grocery stores.

Dim Sum: Delicacies served in Chinese tea houses. Small items ranging from dumplings to desserts are brought to the table in steamer baskets or on individual plates for diners to make their own choices.

Dried Shiitake (shee-TAH-kay) **Mushrooms:** Originally from Japan, these mushrooms are used in soups and other dishes to impart a deep beef-like flavor.

Fish Sauce: Made from salty liquid and fermented fish. A pungent and strongly accented sauce that lends a unique briny flavor without the fish taste. Found in Asian section of grocery stores.

Ghee (GEE): Butter that has been heated to separate and to clarify it, then cooked longer to evaporate any liquid. The remaining solids are browned slightly and have a nutty, caramel flavor and aroma. Ghee has a higher smoking point than regular butter, making it excellent for frying. Vegetable ghee, made from canola oil, is readily found in the Asian section of grocery stores.

Hoisin (HOY-sihn) **Sauce:** Sweet and spicy mixture of soybeans, garlic, chili peppers and spices. Found in Asian section of grocery stores.

Japanese Wine: See Mirin.

Kaffir Lime Leaves: Leaves that look like two leaves joined end to end. Used whole in soups and curries to add flavor, then removed. Most easily found in the frozen food section of large grocery stores.

Konbu (KHON-boo): Seasoned seaweed sold in sheets to wrap sushi, or shredded into dashi to use in soups. Found in Asian grocery stores.

Lemon Grass: Asian herb with sour lemon flavor and fragrance. Looks like a large green onion, except yellow and gray. Only the inside and bottom 6 inches (15 cm) are used. The dry straw-like pieces are removed and discarded before using in recipes. A generous strip of lemon peel can be used as a substitute for one stalk of lemon grass.

Masala (mah-SAH-lah): Indian spice blend with numerous variations of at least 10 spices. Used for flavoring curries and other dishes, Indian cooks generally have their own favorite masala. North Americans can buy the most common types in Asian section of grocery stores.

Ingredient Glossary

Mirin (MIHR-ihn): Low alcohol, sweet golden cooking seasoning made from glutinous rice. Found in Asian section of grocery stores.

Miso (MEE-soh): Also called fermented soybean paste or bean paste. Has the texture of peanut butter but comes in a variety of flavors and colors. The darker the color, the more intense the flavor. Japanese seasoning used as a condiment and in sauces, dips, soups, marinades and salad dressings. Found in Asian grocery stores.

Nori (NOH-ree) **Sheets:** Sweet-tasting paper-thin sheets of dried seaweed used for wrapping sushi and rice balls, or as a seasoning or garnish. Unroasted nori is a deep burgundy in color; roasted nori is green. Can be ground up and added to sushi rice or soup. Found in Asian section of grocery stores.

Oyster Sauce: Thick dark brown sauce made from oysters, brine and soy sauce. Found in Asian section of grocery stores.

Rice Flour: Made from regular white rice. Used for baking or as a thickening agent.

Rice Stick Noodles: Translucent noodles, about 1/4 inch (6 mm) wide, made of rice flour. Found in Asian section of grocery stores.

Rice Vinegar: Chinese and Japanese vinegar made from fermented rice. Milder than North American vinegar. Chinese rice vinegars come in white for sweet-and-sour dishes, red as a condiment for boiled or steamed crab and black as a table sauce. Japanese rice vinegar is used in salads and sushi rice. Found in Asian section of grocery stores.

Sake (SAH-kee): Japanese wine made from fermented steamed rice. Used in sauces and marinades or as a beverage. Unlike regular red or white wine, sake is served hot from a jug and poured into tiny cups (or small liqueur glasses). A guest never pours his or her own, instead they hold their cup towards the host to indicate that they would like some. To heat sake, place an open bottle in a saucepan with water. Heat on stove top until water is simmering. Remove from heat and let sit several minutes before pouring. Found in liquor stores.

Sambal Oelek (SAHM-bahl OH-lehk): Also called chili paste. This condiment for rice and curries is a mixture of chilies, brown sugar and salt. Found in Asian section of grocery stores.

Shrimp Paste: Made of ground, salted, fermented shrimp. Has a strong fishy flavor and is used sparingly. Sold in compressed cakes ranging from soft and grayish-pink to firm and brownish in color. Found in Asian grocery stores.

Somen (SOH-mehn) **Noodles:** Thin, white, wheat flour noodles used in Japanese cooking. Found in Asian grocery stores.

Suey Choy (Chinese cabbage): Grows in heads. The leaves are thinner, crisper and milder tasting than regular cabbage. Also called napa cabbage or celery cabbage.

Sushi (SOO-shee): Japanese specialty made with rice vinegar-flavored rice and a variety of additional ingredients from raw fish to julienned vegetables. Generally rolled in nori sheets and sliced to make small rounds.

Thai Chili Peppers: Small, very thin, very hot red or green chili peppers.

Wasabi (WAH-sah-bee) **Paste:** Also called Japanese horseradish. Green paste or powder that is sharp, hot tasting and used very sparingly. Found in Asian section of grocery stores.

Wrappers: Dough rolled very thin and cut into squares. Used for egg rolls, spring rolls, dumplings and won tons. Can be bought in various thicknesses and shapes. Also comes in white rice paper wrappers made from a mixture of water and a part of the rice-paper plant. Found in the freezer section or produce section of grocery stores.

Japanese Omelet (Japan)

Cold sweet egg sounds unusual, but you'll be pleasantly surprised by the taste sensation. Garnish with something really colorful (see Garnishes, page 11) to contrast the pale egg.

Large eggs	3	3
Water	3 tbsp.	50 mL
Granulated sugar	3 tbsp.	50 mL
Mirin (Japanese sweet cooking seasoning)	1 tbsp.	15 mL
Salt, sprinkle		

Combine all 5 ingredients in small bowl. Divide into 3 equal portions. Grease non-stick 12 inch (30 cm) frying pan with cooking spray. Pour in first portion of egg mixture. Cook, without stirring, on medium-low until almost set. Roll up, jelly roll-style, starting at edge closest to you. Without removing egg, grease pan. Add second portion of egg mixture. Gently lift rolled egg to allow some egg mixture underneath. Cook until almost set. Roll rolled egg towards you, gently gathering second amount of egg mixture around rolled egg. Without removing rolled egg, grease pan. Add third portion of egg mixture. Gently lift rolled egg to allow some egg mixture underneath. Cook until almost set. Roll away from you, gently gathering third amount of egg mixture around rolled egg, forming 1 roll of 3 separately cooked "omelets." To make traditional ridges, immediately place roll on bamboo mat and roll tightly, yet gently. Cool. Chill until ready to serve. Remove bamboo mat. Cuts into 10 slices. Makes 10 appetizers or serves 2 as a first course.

1 appetizer: 39 Calories; 1.5 g Total Fat; 19 mg Sodium; 2 g Protein; 4 g Carbohydrate; 0 g Dietary Fiber

Variation: May be served warm as a meal. Do not roll in bamboo mat.

Paré Pointer

He was given a new boomerang and has spent two days trying to get rid of the old one.

Appetizers

Pajeon (Korea)

Pah-JUHN are also called Green Onion Pancakes. Some form of "jeon" or
pancake is enjoyed as a snack food by Koreans at any time of day.
Serve with Dipping Sauce, page 117, or Nuoc Cham, page 121.

Large eggs	2	2
Onion powder	1/2 tsp.	2 mL
Finely chopped gingerroot (or 1/8 tsp., 0.5 mL, ground ginger)	1/2 tsp.	2 mL
Garlic powder	1/4 tsp.	1 mL
Water	1 cup	250 mL
Sesame (or cooking) oil	1 tsp.	5 mL
All-purpose flour	1 cup	250 mL
Rice flour	1/3 cup	75 mL
Salt	1 tsp.	5 mL
Cayenne pepper	1/8 tsp.	0.5 mL
Water, approximately	1 tbsp.	15 mL
Finely sliced green onion	3/4 cup	175 mL
Finely diced red pepper	2 tbsp.	30 mL
Chopped cooked salad shrimp (about 8 oz., 225 g)	2/3 cup	150 mL
Cooking oil, approximately	1 tbsp.	15 mL

Beat first 10 ingredients together in medium bowl until smooth.

Stir in second amount of water, 1 tsp. (5 mL) at a time, until consistency of
medium batter. Let stand for 10 minutes.

Add green onion, red pepper and shrimp. Stir.

Heat 1 tsp. (5 mL) cooking oil in large non-stick frying pan until hot. Add
about 2 tbsp. (30 mL) batter for each pancake. Cook on medium for
1 minute until edges begin to appear dry. Turn over. Cook until golden.
Repeat with remaining batter, using cooking oil to prevent sticking as
necessary. Makes 20 pancakes.

1 pancake: 57 Calories; 1.6 g Total Fat; 137 mg Sodium; 3 g Protein; 8 g Carbohydrate;
trace Dietary Fiber

Pictured on page 18.

Pakora (India)

Pah-KOOR-ah is the Punjabi name for "fritters." Serve as a snack or appetizer with Coriander Chutney, page 37, or Cucumber Raita, page 38.

Whole wheat flour	2/3 cup	150 mL
Salt	1/2 tsp.	2 mL
Cayenne pepper	1/4 tsp.	1 mL
Finely chopped fresh cilantro (or parsley)	2 tsp.	10 mL
Water, approximately	3/4 cup	175 mL
Fresh vegetable pieces (such as onion slices, pepper chunks, cauliflower and broccoli florets, zucchini chunks), patted dry	3 cups	750 mL

Cooking oil, for deep-frying

Combine flour, salt, cayenne pepper and cilantro in medium bowl. Stir in water. Add more water, 1 tsp. (5 mL) at a time, until consistency of medium-stiff batter.

Fold vegetable pieces into batter until well coated.

Remove vegetable pieces, 1 at a time, from batter. Cook, a few at a time, in hot (375°F, 190°C) cooking oil in deep-fryer or large saucepan for about 2 minutes until golden. Remove to paper towels to drain. Makes about 32 pieces. Serves 6.

1 serving: 172 Calories; 12.7 g Total Fat; 206 mg Sodium; 3 g Protein; 14 g Carbohydrate; 3 g Dietary Fiber

1. Kujolp'an, page 20 (Korea)
   a) Beef tenderloin steak
   b) Cabbage Kimchee, page 33 (Korea)
   c) Green onion
   d) Egg whites
   e) Carrots
   f) Brown mushrooms
   g) English cucumber
   h) Bamboo shoots
   i) Shrimp
   j) Pancakes
2. Dipping Sauce, page 117 (Korea)

Props Courtesy Of: Cherison Enterprises Inc.
Pier 1 Imports
Stokes

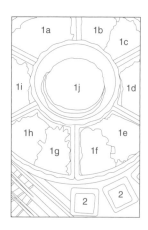

Surprise Crab Cakes (Vietnam)

These cute cakes are even better when dipped in Lime Ginger Sauce, page 120.

Cans of crabmeat (4 1/4 oz., 120 g, each), drained and cartilage removed	2	2
All-purpose flour	1 1/2 cups	375 mL
Water	1 1/2 cups	375 mL
Salt	1/2 tsp.	2 mL
Pepper	1/8 tsp.	0.5 mL
Medium potato, peeled and cut into very thin strips and then in half (or coarsely grated)	1	1
Green onion, chopped	1	1
Fish sauce	1 tsp.	5 mL
Raw large shrimp (about 50), peeled and deveined (see Tip, page 86)	3/4 lb.	340 g
Cooking oil, for deep-frying		

Place crab in food processor. Process until paste-like consistency.

Stir flour into water in medium bowl until smooth. Add salt, pepper and crab. Stir well.

Add potato, green onion and fish sauce. Stir.

Place about 1 tbsp. (15 mL) batter in small shallow bowl. Swirl shrimp in batter, leaving tail uncoated. Scrape shrimp and batter with rubber spatula into hot (375°F, 190°C) cooking oil in wok. Deep-fry, turning over once, until golden. Repeat with remaining batter and shrimp. Makes 50 crab cakes.

1 crab cake: 67 Calories; 4.8 g Total Fat; 72 mg Sodium; 2 g Protein; 4 g Carbohydrate; trace Dietary Fiber

Pictured on page 125.

1. Pajeon (Green Onion Pancakes), page 15 (Korea)
2. Meatballs With Chutney Sauce, page 64 (Asia)
3. Thai Pizza On A Garlic Crust, page 66 (Thailand)
4. Nuoc Cham (Chili Dipping Sauce), page 121 (Vietnam)

Props Courtesy Of: Mikasa Home Store

Kujolp'an (Korea)

Kuh-JUHL-pahn is the lacquered serving dish used to hold pancakes in the center bowl and fillings in the surrounding bowls. Fillings can be made ahead and chilled until ready to serve.

PANCAKE BATTER

All-purpose flour	1 1/2 cups	375 mL
Salt	1/2 tsp.	2 mL
Pepper (white is best)	1/8 tsp.	0.5 mL
Large eggs	2	2
Milk	1 cup	250 mL
Cold water	1 cup	250 mL

Pancake Batter: Combine flour, salt and pepper in medium bowl. Make a well in center. Add eggs, milk and cold water to well. Beat on high until smooth. Let stand for 30 minutes. Batter should be fairly thin. Add 2 tbsp. (30 mL) batter to hot 6 inch (15 cm) greased non-stick frying pan, immediately tilting pan to cover bottom completely. Cook for 15 seconds. Turn over. Cook for about 15 seconds until firm but not brown. Remove pancake to plate to cool before stacking. Makes about 25 pancakes.

FILLINGS

1. Can of bamboo shoots, drained and cut julienne	8 oz.	227 mL
Granulated sugar	1 tsp.	5 mL
Sesame (or cooking) oil	1 tsp.	5 mL

Sauté bamboo shoots and sugar in hot sesame oil in frying pan until bamboo shoots are slightly softened. Makes about 1 cup (250 mL).

2. Green onions, cut into 2 inch (5 cm) pieces and thinly sliced lengthwise	5	5
Sesame (or cooking) oil	1 tsp.	5 mL

Sauté green onion in hot sesame oil in frying pan until slightly softened. Makes about 3/4 cup (175 mL).

3. Raw medium shrimp, peeled, deveined and chopped	6 oz.	170 g
Salt, sprinkle		
Lemon juice	2 tbsp.	30 mL
Sesame (or cooking) oil	1 tsp.	5 mL

Sauté first 3 ingredients in hot sesame oil in frying pan until shrimp is pink. Makes about 1 cup (250 mL).

(continued on next page)

4. Cabbage Kimchee, page 33 (or commercial)	2/3 cup	150 mL

Drain and blot kimchee as dry as possible between paper towels. Cut into small pieces if necessary. Makes 2/3 cup (150 mL).

5. Fresh brown mushrooms, sliced	2 cups	500 mL
Garlic clove, minced	1	1
Soy sauce	1 tbsp.	15 mL
Sesame (or cooking) oil	1 tsp.	5 mL

Sauté first 3 ingredients in hot sesame oil in frying pan until liquid has evaporated. Makes about 1/2 cup (125 mL).

Variation: Omit mushrooms and garlic. Add 2 medium carrots, cut julienne, and sprinkle of salt. Makes about 3/4 cup (175 mL).

6. Soy sauce	2 tsp.	10 mL
Sliced green onion	1 tbsp.	15 mL
Sesame seeds, toasted	1 tsp.	5 mL
Garlic clove, minced	1	1
Granulated sugar	1 tsp.	5 mL
Beef tenderloin steak, partially frozen, sliced paper-thin	4 oz.	113 g
Sesame (or cooking) oil	1 tsp.	5 mL

Stir first 5 ingredients in small bowl. Add beef. Stir. Marinate for 10 minutes. Sauté beef and marinade in hot sesame oil in frying pan until beef reaches desired doneness. Makes 1/2 cup (125 mL).

7. Egg whites (large), fork-beaten	4	4
Salt, sprinkle		

Cook 1/2 each of egg white and salt in greased non-stick frying pan for about 2 minutes, turning over once, until firm. Roll up. Cut crosswise into thin shreds. Repeat with remaining egg white and salt. Makes about 3/4 cup (175 mL).

To serve, place all fillings in either small serving bowls or individual bowls of Kujolp'an. Carefully peel off pancake. Fill with your choice of filling. Fold in sides. Roll to enclose filling. Dip pancakes in Dipping Sauce, page 117. Serves 8.

1 serving: 224 Calories; 6.5 g Total Fat; 515 mg Sodium; 16 g Protein; 26 g Carbohydrate; 2 g Dietary Fiber

Variation: Combine 2/3 cup (150 mL) julienned English cucumber, with peel; 1 tbsp. (15 mL) rice vinegar and 1 tsp. (5 mL) granulated sugar in small bowl. Makes 1/2 cup (125 mL).

Pictured on page 17.

Sushi Rice (Japan)

This is a basic sushi rice that can be used as is or with added color and flavor in Sushi Stacks, page 23, Whirl-A-Gig Sushi, page 24, Sushi Lettuce Boats, page 25, or Rainbow Sushi, page 27.

Short grain white rice	1 1/2 cups	375 mL
Water, to cover		
Water	2 cups	500 mL
Rice (or white) vinegar	3 tbsp.	50 mL
Granulated sugar	2 tbsp.	30 mL
Salt	1 tsp.	5 mL
Mirin (Japanese sweet cooking seasoning)	3 tbsp.	50 mL

Rinse rice in cold water until water is no longer cloudy. Cover rice with first amount of water in medium bowl. Let stand for 30 minutes. Drain.

Combine rice and second amount of water in medium saucepan. Bring to a boil on high. Reduce heat to very low. Cover. Simmer for 20 minutes without lifting lid. Remove from heat. Let stand for 10 minutes without lifting lid.

Combine rice vinegar, sugar, salt and mirin in small bowl. Stir until sugar is dissolved. Add to rice. Stir. Cool. Makes 4 cups (1 L).

1/2 cup (125 mL): 164 Calories; 0.2 g Total Fat; 298 mg Sodium; 3 g Protein; 36 g Carbohydrate; 0 g Dietary Fiber

PARSLEY SUSHI RICE: Add 3 tbsp. (50 mL) chopped fresh parsley or nori flakes to cooked Sushi Rice. Stir. (To make nori flakes, process 1 torn nori sheet in blender until consistency of flakes.)

PINK SUSHI RICE: Combine 3/4 to 1 cup (175 to 250 mL) beet juice (from canned beets) and enough water to equal 2 cups (500 mL). Cook rice in liquid.

YELLOW SUSHI RICE: Add 1 tsp. (5 mL) turmeric to rice and water before cooking rice.

Appetizers

Sushi Stacks (Japan)

Neat and nutritious Japanese finger food. Feel free to switch white and yellow rice layers. Just remember that the second rice layer needs to be double the amount of the first rice layer. Can be served on round rice crackers.

Cooked Yellow Sushi Rice, page 22	1 cup	250 mL
Can of red salmon, drained, skin and round bones removed	7 1/2 oz.	213 g
Lemon juice	1 tsp.	5 mL
Prepared horseradish	1 tsp.	5 mL
Onion powder	1/4 tsp.	1 mL
Liquid smoke	1/8 tsp.	0.5 mL
Salt	1/8 tsp.	0.5 mL
Mayonnaise	2 tbsp.	30 mL
Cooked Sushi Rice, page 22	2 cups	500 mL
Paper-thin small radish slices, for garnish	36	36
Fresh chives (or green onions, slivered), for garnish	12	12

Lay sheet of plastic wrap loosely over 12 cup mini-muffin pan. Press 1 1/2 tsp. (7 mL) yellow rice firmly into each cup, pushing down plastic wrap.

Mash next 7 ingredients together well with fork on large plate. Place 1 1/2 tsp. (7 mL) on each rice layer. Spread evenly.

Firmly place 1 tbsp. (15 mL) white rice on each salmon layer. Invert muffin pan onto flat surface. Remove pan. Gently remove plastic wrap.

Garnish with radish and chives. Makes 12 sushi stacks.

1 sushi stack: 145 Calories; 2.7 g Total Fat; 295 mg Sodium; 4 g Protein; 24 g Carbohydrate; trace Dietary Fiber

Pictured on front cover.

Paré Pointer
If you kept pampering your cow, would you get spoiled milk?

Whirl-A-Gig Sushi (Japan)

This vegetarian version of a Japanese classic is a rainbow of taste.

Nori (roasted seaweed) sheets	2	2
Cooked Sushi Rice, page 22	2 cups	500 mL
Wasabi paste (Japanese horseradish)	1 tsp.	5 mL
Frozen whole green beans, cooked	1/2 cup	125 mL
Small carrot, cut into 4 inch (10 cm) matchsticks, cooked	1	1
Can of sliced beets (14 oz., 398 mL, size), drained, cut julienne and patted dry with paper towel	1/2	1/2

Place first nori sheet on bamboo rolling mat. Dampen 1/2 inch (12 mm) along 1 edge of long side. Lay second nori sheet overlapping dampened edge, extending beyond mat. Spread rice over nori sheets, using wet fork, almost to edge on 3 sides. Leave 2 inches (5 cm) without rice on edge farthest away from you.

Very thinly spread with wasabi paste. Make 6 equally-spaced rows with remaining 3 ingredients, using 1/2 of each per row, on rice. Starting at edge nearest to you, roll up snugly, using mat to assist. Cover with plastic wrap. Chill. Cuts into 8 slices.

1 slice: 99 Calories; 0.2 g Total Fat; 229 mg Sodium; 2 g Protein; 21 g Carbohydrate; 1 g Dietary Fiber

Pictured on front cover.

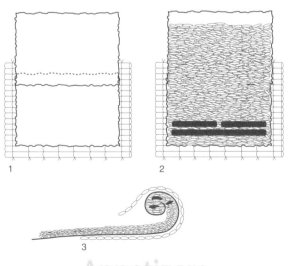

Sushi Lettuce Boats (Japan)

Eye-pleasing appetizers that are as delicious as they look.

Cooked Sushi Rice, page 22	1 1/2 cups	375 mL
Small green (or red) leaf lettuce leaves	3	3
Small butter lettuce leaves	3	3
Radicchio leaves	3	3
Small Belgian endive leaves	3	3
TOPPINGS		
Smoked salmon (or trout) slices	3	3
Capers, drained and rinsed	3	3
Radish slices	3	3
Finely grated carrot	1 1/2 tsp.	7 mL
Paper-thin cucumber slices	3	3
Caviar	1 1/2 tsp.	7 mL
Fresh chives	2	2
Fresh dill sprigs	2	2

Shape rice, with damp hands, into 12 balls or egg shapes, using 2 tbsp. (30 mL) rice for each. Place in center of your choice of leaves.

Toppings: Arrange your choice of the remaining 8 ingredients in different combinations over rice. Chill. Makes 12 boats.

1 green leaf lettuce with 1 slice smoked salmon: 75 Calories; 1 g Total Fat; 599 mg Sodium; 4 g Protein; 11 g Carbohydrate; trace Dietary Fiber

Pictured on page 144.

 tip Don't put too much soy sauce on your sushi. The rice will fall apart and the taste of the sauce will dominate. Finally, to get the full benefit of all the flavors, always place sushi in the mouth so the topping encounters the tongue first.

Vegetable Samosas (India)

These will be the first to disappear! Serve warm with
Coriander Chutney, page 37, or Date Chutney, page 41.

FILLING

Chopped onion	3/4 cup	175 mL
Green chili pepper, finely chopped	1	1
Cooking oil	1 tbsp.	15 mL
Ground cumin	1/4 tsp.	1 mL
Turmeric	1/8 tsp.	0.5 mL
Chopped cabbage	1 cup	250 mL
Grated carrot	1/3 cup	75 mL
Medium potato, peeled and cut into 1 inch (2.5 cm) cubes	1	1
Frozen peas	1 cup	250 mL
Chicken bouillon powder	1/2 tsp.	2 mL
Water	1/3 cup	75 mL
Garam Masala, page 40 (or commercial)	1/2 tsp.	2 mL
Plain yogurt	2 tbsp.	30 mL
Salt	1/4 tsp.	1 mL
Frozen phyllo pastry sheets, thawed according to package directions	12	12
Ghee, melted	1/2 cup	125 mL

Filling: Sauté onion and chili pepper in cooking oil in medium saucepan for about 5 minutes, stirring occasionally, until onion is soft.

Add next 8 ingredients. Stir. Cover. Cook on medium-low for 20 minutes, stirring occasionally. Add more water, 1 tbsp. (15 mL) at a time, if necessary to prevent vegetables from sticking to bottom of pan. Cabbage should be very soft and potatoes broken up.

Stir in Garam Masala, yogurt and salt. Cool to room temperature. Makes 2 cups (500 mL) filling.

(continued on next page)

Appetizers

Lay 1 phyllo sheet on work surface. Lightly brush with ghee. Keep remaining phyllo sheets covered with wet tea towel to prevent drying out. Fold phyllo sheet into thirds towards middle. Lightly brush top with ghee. Place 2 1/2 tbsp. (37 mL) filling in center at 1 end. Fold 1 corner diagonally towards straight edge to form triangle. Continue folding back and forth in same fashion, enclosing filling. Repeat with remaining phyllo sheets, ghee and filling. Place on ungreased baking sheet. Bake in 400°F (205°C) oven for about 12 minutes until golden. Makes 12 samosas.

1 samosa: 167 Calories; 10.5 g Total Fat; 282 mg Sodium; 3 g Protein; 16 g Carbohydrate; 1 g Dietary Fiber

Rainbow Sushi (Japan)

A pretty sushi that serves a crowd.
See the Variation, below, to make a smaller batch.

Cooked Parsley Sushi Rice, page 22	4 cups	1 L
Cooked Pink Sushi Rice, page 22	4 cups	1 L
Cooked Yellow Sushi Rice, page 22	4 cups	1 L

Lotus root slices (parboiled and
  cooled), for garnish
Baby carrot, cut into paper-thin
  slices, for garnish
Okra slices, for garnish
Non-fat plain yogurt, for garnish

Spoon Parsley Sushi Rice into foil-lined 9 x 13 inch (22 x 33 cm) pan. Spread and firmly press evenly in bottom of pan using wet fork or small spatula. Repeat with Pink Sushi Rice and Yellow Sushi Rice. Cover with plastic wrap. Firmly press all 3 layers together. Chill for at least 3 hours. Cut into 1 x 1 inch (2.5 x 2.5 cm) pieces.

Decorate with your choice of garnishes. Cuts into about 100 pieces.

1 piece: 39 Calories; 0.1 g Total Fat; 72 mg Sodium; 1 g Protein; 9 g Carbohydrate; trace Dietary Fiber

Variation: For a smaller batch, halve the rice recipe and press into greased 8 x 8 inch (20 x 20 cm) pan. Cuts into 64 pieces.

Deep-Fried Spring Rolls (Vietnam)

Fabulous! Traditionally placed in a lettuce leaf with fresh mint. Serve with Miso Dipping Sauce, page 117, or Spring Roll Dipping Sauce, page 118.

Lean ground pork	1 lb.	454 g
Raw medium shrimp (about 1 cup, 250 mL), peeled, deveined and chopped (see Tip, page 86)	8 oz.	225 g
Large egg, fork-beaten	1	1
Green onions, finely chopped	3	3
Chopped fresh bean sprouts	1 cup	250 mL
Finely grated carrot	2 tbsp.	30 mL
Chopped fresh parsley (or 1 1/2 tsp., 7 mL, flakes)	2 tbsp.	30 mL
Salt	1/2 tsp.	2 mL
Pepper, sprinkle		
Package of bean threads (4 oz., 110 g, size) or rice stick noodles	1/3	1/3
Boiling water, to cover		
Large rice paper rounds	23	23
Hot water		
Cooking oil, for deep-frying		

Combine first 9 ingredients in large bowl.

Cover bean threads with boiling water in small bowl. Let stand for about 2 minutes until softened. Drain. Cut into 3 to 4 inch (7.5 to 10 cm) lengths. Add to pork mixture. Stir.

Soak each rice paper round in hot water in shallow pie plate for 30 to 40 seconds until softened. Lay on cutting board. Cut into quarters. Lay 1 piece flat, point away from you. Lay another piece on top leaving 1 1/2 to 2 inches (3.8 to 5 cm) of first piece showing (see Figure 1, next page). Spoon 1 tbsp. (15 mL) filling onto center of rice paper. Starting with bottom curved edge, roll to enclose filling, tucking in sides. Repeat with remaining rice papers and filling. Cover with wet tea towel to prevent drying out.

Cook spring rolls, a few at a time, in hot (375°F, 190°C) cooking oil in large wok or deep-fryer for 6 to 8 minutes, turning at halftime, until deep golden. Remove to paper towels to drain. Makes 46 spring rolls.

(continued on next page)

1 spring roll: 56 Calories; 3.5 g Total Fat; 41 mg Sodium; 3 g Protein; 3 g Carbohydrate; trace Dietary Fiber

Pictured on page 125.

To Make Ahead: Spring rolls can be deep-fried and then frozen. To reheat from frozen state, place on ungreased baking sheet. Bake in 350°F (175°C) oven for 20 minutes until heated through.

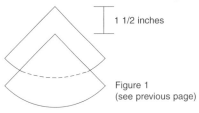

1 1/2 inches

Figure 1
(see previous page)

Vietnamese Spring Rolls (Vietnam)

Golden brown, crusty and crispy pastry with a moist pork and vegetable filling.
Dip in Spring Roll Dipping Sauce, page 118, or Nuoc Leo, page 120.

Lean ground pork	1 lb.	454 g
Finely grated carrot	1 cup	250 mL
Rice vermicelli, cooked	1/2 cup	125 mL
Soy sauce	1 tbsp.	15 mL
Oyster sauce	1 tbsp.	15 mL
Garlic clove, minced (or 1/4 tsp., 1 mL, powder)	1	1
Finely chopped gingerroot (or 1/4 tsp., 1 mL, ground ginger)	1 tsp.	5 mL
Green onions, finely chopped	2	2
Large egg, fork-beaten	1	1
Spring roll wrappers (6 inch, 15 cm, size)	25	25

Cooking oil, for deep-frying

Mix first 9 ingredients well in large bowl.

Place about 2 tbsp. (30 mL) filling in center of each spring roll wrapper. Fold up 1 corner over filling. Fold in both sides. Dampen edge of wrapper. Roll tightly to seal. Repeat with remaining filling and wrappers.

Deep-fry in hot (375°F, 190°C) cooking oil in large wok or deep-fryer for about 5 minutes, turning at halftime, until golden. Makes 25 spring rolls.

1 spring roll: 174 Calories; 6.9 g Total Fat; 290 mg Sodium; 7 g Protein; 21 g Carbohydrate; trace Dietary Fiber

Chicken Tikka (India)

These are satay-like kabobs with a spicy yogurt coating. They are similar to
Tandoori cooked food in flavor when grilled over a hot barbecue.
Serve with Date Chutney, page 41, or a fruit chutney.

MARINADE		
Garlic cloves, minced (or 3/4 tsp., 4 mL, powder)	3	3
Finely chopped gingerroot (or 1/4 tsp., 1 mL, ground ginger)	1 tsp.	5 mL
Lemon juice	1 tbsp.	15 mL
Paprika	2 tsp.	10 mL
Chili powder	2 tsp.	10 mL
Garam Masala, page 40 (or commercial)	2 tsp.	10 mL
Plain yogurt	2/3 cup	150 mL
Boneless, skinless chicken breast halves (about 5), cut into 1 inch (2.5 cm) cubes	1 1/4 lbs.	560 g
Bamboo skewers (4 inch, 10 cm, length), soaked in water for 10 minutes	16	16

Marinade: Combine first 7 ingredients in medium non-metal bowl. Makes
3/4 cup (175 mL).

Add chicken. Stir until well coated. Cover. Marinate in refrigerator for at least
6 hours or overnight, stirring several times. Remove chicken. Discard
marinade.

Thread about 3 pieces of chicken onto each skewer. Grill over medium-high
heat for 8 to 9 minutes, turning several times, until no longer pink inside.
Makes about 16 kabobs.

1 kabob: 49 Calories; 0.9 g Total Fat; 11 mg Sodium; 9 g Protein; 2 g Carbohydrate;
trace Dietary Fiber

Variation: Instead of making kabobs, use 1 1/2 lbs. (680 g), about
30, chicken drumettes, skin removed. Poke fleshy part of drumette several
times with point of sharp knife before marinating. Grill over medium-high
heat for about 20 minutes, turning several times, until no longer pink
inside.

Pleated Purses (Thailand)

These appetizers are time consuming and a bit fussy, but you'll get rave reviews.
Serve with Peanut Sauce, page 119, or Lime Ginger Sauce, page 120.

Chives, 4 inches (10 cm) in length (or green onion, slivered)	20	20
Boiling water		

FILLING

Lean ground pork	2 oz.	57 g
Raw medium shrimp (fresh or frozen, thawed), peeled, deveined and finely chopped (see Tip, page 86)	5 1/2 oz.	154 g
Finely grated gingerroot (or 1/8 tsp., 0.5 mL, ground ginger)	1/2 tsp.	2 mL
Garlic clove, crushed (or 1/4 tsp., 1 mL, powder)	1	1
Lemon juice	1 1/2 tsp.	7 mL
Salt	1/2 tsp.	2 mL
Ground coriander	1/4 tsp.	1 mL
Freshly ground pepper, sprinkle		
Cornstarch	2 tsp.	10 mL
Spring roll wrappers (6 inch, 15 cm, size)	20	20

Cooking oil, for deep-frying

Plunge chives into boiling water for about 15 seconds until softened.

Filling: Combine first 9 ingredients in small bowl. Makes 1 cup (250 mL) filling.

Mound about 1 1/2 tsp. (7 mL) filling to 1 side of center on spring roll wrapper. Fold wrapper diagonally in half. Pleat edges above the filling by folding accordion-style. Hold together. Wrap chive twice around the pleated portion of wrapper at top of filling. Carefully tie in a knot. The filling should be enclosed in a little "purse." Trim chive with scissors. Repeat with remaining filling and wrappers, keeping wrappers and filled purses covered with a damp tea towel to prevent drying out.

Deep-fry, 3 to 4 purses at a time, in hot (375°F, 190°C) cooking oil in large saucepan or deep-fryer for 2 minutes, turning several times, until golden. Remove with slotted spoon to paper towels to drain. Tip purse so cooking oil drains out of pleated portion. Makes 20 purses.

1 purse: 137 Calories; 4.2 g Total Fat; 256 mg Sodium; 5 g Protein; 19 g Carbohydrate; trace Dietary Fiber

Appetizers

Battered Meatballs (Korea)

*Very lightly textured. A mild flavor that goes with
a variety of sauces, such as Dipping Sauce, page 117.*

Lean ground pork	1/2 lb.	225 g
Package of firm tofu, drained well and cut into 1 inch (2.5 cm) cubes	12 1/3 oz.	350 g
Large egg	1	1
Soy sauce	1 tbsp.	15 mL
Cayenne pepper	1/4 tsp.	1 mL
Garlic cloves, minced (or 3/4 tsp., 4 mL, powder)	3	3
Green onions, finely sliced	2	2
Sesame seeds, toasted (see Tip, page 63)	2 tsp.	10 mL
All-purpose flour	1/3 cup	75 mL
Seasoned salt	1/2 tsp.	2 mL
Freshly ground pepper, sprinkle		
Large eggs	2	2
Milk (or water)	2 tsp.	10 mL
Cooking oil	2 tbsp.	30 mL

Place first 5 ingredients in food processor. Process for 3 to 4 minutes until
moist and smooth. Turn into medium bowl.

Add garlic, green onion and sesame seeds. Mix. Shape into 1 inch (2.5 cm)
balls.

Combine flour, seasoned salt and pepper in small bowl.

Beat second amount of eggs and milk together in separate small bowl.

Heat cooking oil in large non-stick frying pan until hot. Roll meatballs in
flour mixture and then dip in egg mixture to coat completely. Fry in frying
pan for 8 to 9 minutes, turning frequently, until well browned. Makes
about 50 meatballs.

*1 meatball: 36 Calories; 2.5 g Total Fat; 40 mg Sodium; 2 g Protein; 1 g Carbohydrate;
trace Dietary Fiber*

Cabbage Kimchee (Korea)

This is the most commonly offered KIHM-chee. Korean people will have this with breakfast, lunch and dinner. In North America, it also makes a good appetizer with beer. Use in Kujolp'an, page 20.

Suey choy (Chinese cabbage)	1 1/2 lbs.	680 g
Coarse (pickling) salt	1/2 cup	125 mL
Water	5 cups	1.25 L
Water	1/2 cup	125 mL
Apple cider vinegar	1/4 cup	60 mL
Fish sauce	2 tbsp.	30 mL
Granulated sugar	1 tbsp.	15 mL
Garlic cloves, minced (or 3/4 tsp., 4 mL, powder)	3	3
Finely grated gingerroot (or 1/4 tsp., 1 mL, ground ginger)	1 tsp.	5 mL
Paprika	1 tbsp.	15 mL
Cayenne pepper	1/2 tsp.	2 mL

Cut suey choy in half lengthwise. Wash. Drain. Cut each piece in half lengthwise again. Remove hard wedge-shaped core near bottom of each piece. Cut crosswise into 1 1/2 to 2 inch (3.8 to 5 cm) slices. Place in large non-metal bowl. Sprinkle with salt. Toss. Add first amount of water. Let stand for 3 to 4 hours. Drain. Rinse well several times. Squeeze out excess water. Return suey choy to bowl.

Combine remaining 8 ingredients in small bowl. Stir until sugar is dissolved. Add to suey choy. Mix well. Press suey choy into bottom of bowl until liquid forms over surface (see Tip, below). Tightly cover bowl. Let stand at room temperature for 3 to 4 days until suey choy is soured and tangy. Store in jars with tight-fitting lids in refrigerator for up to 2 months. Makes 3 cups (750 mL).

1/4 cup (60 mL): 18 Calories; 0.2 g Total Fat; 762 mg Sodium; 1 g Protein; 4 g Carbohydrate; 1 g Dietary Fiber

For best results when making kimchee, cover vegetables completely with liquid. If liquid does not cover vegetables completely, it may be necessary to stir every so often.

Indian Side Salad (India)

More commonly served as a condiment rather than a salad.
Complements spicy dishes like Punjab Chicken, page 68, or
Chicken Curry Wraps, page 74, since it cools the palate.

Finely chopped tomato	2 cups	500 mL
Diced cucumber	1 cup	250 mL
Sliced green onion	1/4 cup	60 mL
Plain yogurt	1/4 cup	60 mL
Salt	1/2 tsp.	2 mL
Granulated sugar	1/4 tsp.	1 mL
Chopped cilantro (or chopped fresh mint leaves), optional	1 tbsp.	15 mL

Combine tomato and cucumber in sieve. Drain for 15 minutes. Turn into medium bowl.

Add remaining 5 ingredients. Stir. Let stand for 15 minutes to blend flavors. Stir before serving. Makes 3 cups (750 mL).

1/4 cup (60 mL): 14 Calories; 0.2 g Total Fat; 107 mg Sodium; 1 g Protein; 3 g Carbohydrate; 1 g Dietary Fiber

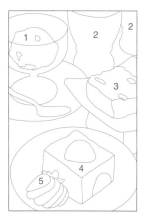

1. Kulfi (East Indian Ice Cream), page 42 (India)
2. Strawberry Lassi, page 46 (India)
3. Gajar Halwa, page 45 (India)
4. Strawberry Snow, page 49 (Japan)
5. Strawberry Fan, page 11

Props Courtesy Of: The Bay
Winners Stores
X/S Wares

Condiments & Spices

Coriander Chutney (India)

In Asia it's called coriander; in North America it's called cilantro.
Whatever you call it, this fresh chutney is delicious.
Great with Pakora, page 16, or Vegetable Samosas, page 26.

Chopped fresh cilantro	1 cup	250 mL
Can of diced green chilies, drained	4 oz.	114 g
Garlic clove (or 1/4 tsp., 1 mL, powder)	1	1
Chopped gingerroot (or 1/2 tsp., 2 mL, ground ginger)	2 tsp.	10 mL
Granulated sugar	2 tsp.	10 mL
Salt	1/2 tsp.	2 mL
Ground cumin	1/8 tsp.	0.5 mL
Cayenne pepper	1/8 tsp.	0.5 mL
Pepper	1/8 tsp.	0.5 mL
Lemon juice	1 tbsp.	15 mL
White vinegar	1 tbsp.	15 mL

Put all 11 ingredients into blender. Process until puréed. Store in airtight container in refrigerator for up to 1 week. Makes 3/4 cup (175 mL).

2 tbsp. (30 mL): 17 Calories; 0.2 g Total Fat; 408 mg Sodium; 1 g Protein; 4 g Carbohydrate; trace Dietary Fiber

Pictured on page 36.

Variation: Add 1/4 cup (60 mL) plain yogurt for a more mellow flavor.

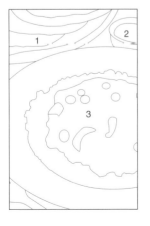

1. Roti, page 123 (India)
2. Coriander Chutney, this page (India)
3. Shrimp Mango Curry, page 86 (Malaysia)

Props Courtesy Of: Artifacts
Dansk Gifts
Pier 1 Imports
The Bay

Cucumber Raita (India)

RI-tah is one of the most common "coolers" to eat with hot spicy foods.
Good with spicy dishes like Pakora, page 16, or Punjab Chicken, page 68.

Plain yogurt	1 cup	250 mL
Ground cumin	1/2 tsp.	2 mL
Salt	1/2 tsp.	2 mL
Paprika	1/2 tsp.	2 mL
Chopped fresh mint leaves	2 tsp.	10 mL
Julienned English cucumber, with peel	3/4 cup	175 mL

Combine first 5 ingredients in medium bowl.

Add cucumber. Mix well. Let stand for 30 minutes to blend flavors. Makes
1 1/2 cups (375 mL).

1 tbsp. (15 mL): 7 Calories; 0.2 g Total Fat; 55 mg Sodium; 1 g Protein; 1 g Carbohydrate;
trace Dietary Fiber

Rosy Ginger Pickle (Japan)

Always served with sushi. Very young gingerroot is best,
but older gingerroot can be used as long as it is still juicy.
The vinegar solution can be used at any time to flavor salads.

Thinly sliced fresh gingerroot	1 cup	250 mL
Boiling water		
Plum vinegar	1/2 cup	125 mL
Mirin (Japanese sweet cooking	3 tbsp.	50 mL
seasoning)		
Salt	1/8 tsp.	0.5 mL
Berry sugar	1/4 cup	60 mL
Sake (rice wine)	2 tbsp.	30 mL

Add ginger to boiling water in medium saucepan. Reduce heat. Simmer for
1 minute. Remove ginger. Discard water.

Combine remaining 5 ingredients in medium bowl until sugar is dissolved.
Add ginger. Stir. Let stand for at least 1 hour. Store in jar with tight-fitting
lid in refrigerator for up to 4 weeks. Makes 1 half pint (1 cup, 250 mL) jar.

3 ginger slices: 27 Calories; 0.1 g Total Fat; 21 mg Sodium; trace Protein; 6 g Carbohydrate;
trace Dietary Fiber

Pictured on front cover.

Oi Kimchee (Korea)

Many varieties of OY KHIM-chee, spicy hot cucumbers,
are served often in Korea.

Water	1 cup	250 mL
Rice flour	4 tsp.	20 mL
Medium English cucumbers, with peel	3	3
Coarse sea salt	1 tbsp.	15 mL
Medium carrot, cut julienne	1	1
Daikon radish (about 1 lb., 454 g), peeled and cut julienne	1	1
Green onions, sliced	5	5
Large red pepper, slivered	1	1
Coarse sea salt	1 tbsp.	15 mL
Fish sauce	1/2 cup	125 mL
Garlic cloves, crushed (or 1 tsp., 5 mL, powder)	4	4
Granulated sugar	1 tbsp.	15 mL
Finely grated gingerroot (or 1/2 tsp., 2 mL, ground ginger)	2 tsp.	10 mL
Dried crushed chilies	1 tbsp.	15 mL

Gradually stir water into rice flour in small saucepan until smooth. Heat and stir on medium-high until boiling and slightly thickened. Cool.

Cut cucumbers in half lengthwise. Cut each piece in half lengthwise again. Cut crosswise into 1/2 inch (12 mm) pieces. Place in large non-metal bowl. Sprinkle with first amount of salt. Toss. Let stand for 30 minutes. Drain.

Add carrot, radish, green onion and red pepper. Toss.

Add remaining 6 ingredients to rice flour mixture. Stir. Add to vegetable mixture. Stir. Serve immediately or store in jar with tight-fitting lid in refrigerator for up to 4 weeks. Makes 12 cups (3 L).

1/4 cup (60 mL): 11 Calories; 0.1 g Total Fat; 406 mg Sodium; 1 g Protein; 2 g Carbohydrate; 1 g Dietary Fiber

Pictured on page 125.

Indian Chai (India)

This sweet, milky spiced tea is one of the best ways to start the day or de-stress at the end of a difficult one.

Milk	3 cups	750 mL
Water	2/3 cup	150 mL
Orange pekoe tea bag	1	1
Cinnamon stick (3 - 4 inches, 7.5 - 10 cm, in length), broken and slightly crushed	1	1
Whole green cardamom, bruised (see Tip, page 41)	8	8
Granulated sugar	1 tbsp.	15 mL
Chopped gingerroot (or 1 1/2 tsp., 7 mL, ground ginger)	2 tbsp.	30 mL
Tea masala	1/2-3/4 tsp.	2-4 mL

Combine all 8 ingredients in large saucepan. Bring to a boil on medium-low, stirring occasionally. Strain into 2 mugs. Makes about 3 cups (750 mL). Serves 2.

1 serving: 201 Calories; 4.3 g Total Fat; 203 mg Sodium; 13 g Protein; 28 g Carbohydrate; trace Dietary Fiber

Garam Masala (India)

Gah-RHAM means "hot" or "warm." Mah-SAH-lah means "mixed spice." Usually added towards the end of the cooking time or right before serving. Use in Vegetable Samosas, page 26, Chicken Tikka, page 30, Date Chutney, page 41, and Punjab Chicken, page 68.

Whole green cardamom, bruised (see Tip, page 41)	2 tbsp.	30 mL
Crushed cinnamon (about four 3 - 4 inch, 7.5 - 10 cm, sticks)	2 tbsp.	30 mL
Whole black peppercorns	2 tsp.	10 mL
Whole cloves	1 tsp.	5 mL
Coriander seed	1/2 tsp.	2 mL
Cumin seed	1/4 tsp.	1 mL

(continued on next page)

Place all 6 ingredients in non-stick frying pan. Heat on low for 7 to 10 minutes, shaking pan or mixing occasionally, until spices become fragrant. Turn out onto plate to cool completely. Grind spices in coffee grinder (see Tip, page 119) or blender until consistency of powder. Makes 1/3 cup (75 mL).

1 tsp. (5 mL): 6 Calories; 0.1 g Total Fat; 1 mg Sodium; trace Protein; 2 g Carbohydrate; trace Dietary Fiber

Date Chutney (India)

This is a substitute for tamarind chutney. Pleasing with Vegetable Samosas, page 26, and Chicken Tikka, page 30.

Chopped dates (1 1/2 cups, 375 mL, lightly packed)	1/2 lb.	225 g
Water	1 cup	250 mL
Lemon juice	3 tbsp.	50 mL
Grated lemon peel	2 tsp.	10 mL
Diced tomato	1/2 cup	125 mL
Brown sugar, packed	1/4 cup	60 mL
White vinegar	1/2 tsp.	2 mL
Garam Masala, page 40 (or commercial)	1/2 tsp.	2 mL
Chili powder	1/4 tsp.	1 mL
Dried crushed chilies	1/8 tsp.	0.5 mL
Ground cumin	1/16 tsp.	0.5 mL

Combine all 11 ingredients in heavy medium saucepan. Cook, uncovered, on medium for about 10 minutes, stirring often, until liquid is almost evaporated. Reduce heat. Cook, uncovered, for about 5 minutes until dates and tomato are reduced to a mush and liquid is absorbed. Makes 2 cups (500 mL).

2 tbsp. (30 mL): 53 Calories; 0.1 g Total Fat; 3 mg Sodium; trace Protein; 14 g Carbohydrate; 1 g Dietary Fiber

 tip *To bruise cardamom, pound cardamom pods with a mallet or press with the flat side of a wide knife to "bruise" or crack them open slightly.*

Kulfi (India)

Pronounced KOOHL-fee, East Indian Ice Cream is always very rich perhaps to cool the palate after a particularly spicy curry. Simply wonderful and so different.

Granulated sugar	3/4 cup	175 mL
Cornstarch	2 tbsp.	30 mL
Cans of evaporated milk (13 1/2 oz., 385 mL, each)	2	2
Whole green cardamom, slightly bruised (see Tip, page 41)	5	5
Egg yolks (large), fork-beaten	3	3
Half-and-half cream	1 1/4 cups	300 mL
Rose water (or 1 tsp., 5 mL, vanilla)	1 tbsp.	15 mL
Egg whites (large)	3	3
Medium coconut, toasted (see Tip, page 63)	1/4 cup	60 mL
Shelled, skinned pistachios, chopped	1/2 cup	125 mL
Chopped golden raisins	1/4 cup	60 mL
Chopped glazed cherries	1/4 cup	60 mL

Combine sugar and cornstarch in large saucepan. Stir in evaporated milk until smooth. Add cardamom. Heat and stir on medium until boiling and slightly thickened.

Stir tablespoonful of milk mixture into egg yolks in small bowl. Gradually stir egg yolk mixture into milk mixture. Cook for 2 to 3 minutes until thickened. Remove from heat. Remove and discard cardamom.

Stir in cream and rose water. Cover with plastic wrap directly on surface to prevent skin from forming. Cool to room temperature.

Beat egg whites in medium bowl until stiff peaks form. Stir into cream mixture.

(continued on next page)

Fold in coconut, pistachios, raisins and cherries. Turn into 9 x 13 inch (22 x 33 cm) pan. Cover with foil. Freeze for 2 hours, stirring edges to center of pan with fork 2 or 3 times. Freeze until firm or freeze in ice-cream maker according to manufacturer's directions. To serve, cut into pieces or scoop with ice-cream scoop. Makes 6 1/2 cups (1.6 L).

1/2 cup (125 mL): 473 Calories; 23.3 g Total Fat; 173 mg Sodium; 14 g Protein; 54 g Carbohydrate; 1 g Dietary Fiber

Pictured on page 35.

Tapioca With Sweet Cherry (Thailand)

Really quick to prepare. This Thai dessert will get rave reviews.

Coconut milk	2 1/2 cups	625 mL
Granulated sugar	2/3 cup	150 mL
Salt	1/8 tsp.	0.5 mL
Large eggs, fork-beaten	2	2
Minute tapioca	1/2 cup	125 mL
Vanilla	1 tsp.	5 mL
Maraschino cherries	6	6
Maraschino cherry syrup (optional)		

Combine first 5 ingredients in large heavy saucepan. Let stand for 30 minutes. Heat and stir on medium for 6 to 8 minutes until boiling. Remove from heat.

Stir in vanilla. Mixture will be only slightly thickened, but will continue to thicken as it cools. Fill 6 individual serving dishes.

Place 1 cherry on top of each. Drizzle with syrup. Cool completely before serving. Makes 3 1/2 cups (875 mL).

1/2 cup (125 mL): 313 Calories; 19.6 g Total Fat; 74 mg Sodium; 4 g Protein; 34 g Carbohydrate; trace Dietary Fiber

Paré Pointer
Actually, a snail is a slug with a crash helmet.

Sweet Banana Pudding (Vietnam)

This dessert will definitely satisfy any craving for sweets!
Vietnamese people traditionally eat fruit for dessert; however,
if a prepared dish is served, it is usually very sweet like this one.

Small pearl tapioca (see Note)	1/4 cup	60 mL
Water	2 cups	500 mL
Firm ripe bananas (see Tip, below), cut into 4 pieces each	6	6
Lemon juice	1 tbsp.	15 mL
Granulated sugar	1 cup	250 mL
Coconut milk	3 cups	750 mL
Bean threads, broken into 1 inch (2.5 cm) pieces	1/2 cup	125 mL
Hot water	1 cup	250 mL
Vanilla	1 tsp.	5 mL

Soak tapioca in water in small bowl overnight. Drain.

Place banana in large saucepan. Sprinkle with lemon juice. Cover with sugar. Let stand for 30 minutes.

Stir in coconut milk and tapioca. Heat and stir on medium-high until just starting to boil. Reduce heat to medium-low. Cover. Simmer for 10 minutes.

Cover bean threads with hot water in separate small bowl. Let stand for 2 minutes. Drain. Add to banana mixture. Stir. Cover. Simmer for about 10 minutes until tapioca is clear. Remove from heat.

Stir in vanilla. Serve hot or cold. Serves 8.

1 serving: 410 Calories; 19.5 g Total Fat; 14 mg Sodium; 3 g Protein; 62 g Carbohydrate; 2 g Dietary Fiber

Note: 2 1/2 tbsp. (37 mL) minute tapioca may be substituted for pearl tapioca. Eliminate soaking step.

To purchase ripe bananas, look for those that are still yellow and firm with brown "freckles" starting to show on the peel. This indicates that the starch is starting to convert to sugar, enhancing the flavor.

Gajar Halwa (India)

"Gajar" is Hindi for "carrot." The texture of gah-JAHR HUHL-wah is unusual but rich and sweet with a wonderful toasted nut flavor.

Ghee	1 tbsp.	15 mL
Chopped almonds, with skin	1/2 cup	125 mL
Chopped shelled pistachios	1/4 cup	60 mL
Ghee	1 tbsp.	15 mL
Grated carrot (about 7 large)	5 cups	1.25 L
Whole green cardamom, bruised (see Tip, page 41)	10	10
Milk	1/2 cup	125 mL
Can of sweetened condensed milk	11 oz.	300 mL
Half-and-half cream (or homogenized milk)	2 cups	500 mL

Heat first amount of ghee in small frying pan until hot. Add almonds and pistachios. Heat and stir on medium for about 2 minutes until toasted. Set aside.

Heat second amount of ghee in large heavy saucepan until hot. Add carrot, cardamom and milk. Heat and stir on medium for about 3 minutes until milk is absorbed.

Stir in condensed milk. Cook, uncovered, on medium-low for about 20 minutes, stirring frequently in beginning and then constantly, until condensed milk is absorbed and carrot starts to turn brown. Remove and discard cardamom.

Add 1/2 of almond mixture. Stir. Heat and stir on low for 3 to 4 minutes until heated through. To serve, place about 1/3 cup (75 mL) in individual serving dishes. Pour 1/4 cup (60 mL) cream over top of each. Divide remaining almond mixture over top of each. Serves 8.

1 serving: 375 Calories; 20.9 g Total Fat; 154 mg Sodium; 10 g Protein; 41 g Carbohydrate; 3 g Dietary Fiber

Variation: Can also be firmly packed into a 9 x 5 x 3 inch (22 x 12.5 x 7.5 cm) loaf pan lined with plastic wrap. Top with reserved almond mixture. Pack firmly. Chill. Cuts into 8 pieces.

Pictured on page 35.

Strawberry Lassi (India)

This is the perfect beverage to cool the body on a hot day or to cool the palate while eating spicy foods. Sources who have visited India report that on the hottest days this was the refreshment of choice!

Plain yogurt	1 cup	250 mL
Cold water	1 1/2 cups	375 mL
Sliced strawberries	1 cup	250 mL
Granulated sugar	2 tsp.	10 mL
Ice cubes	6	6

Put yogurt, cold water, strawberries and sugar into blender. Process until strawberries are smooth.

Process on high, adding ice cubes, 1 at a time, through hole in lid until frothy. Makes 3 2/3 cups (900 mL).

1 cup (250 mL): 67 Calories; 1.3 g Total Fat; 50 mg Sodium; 4 g Protein; 11 g Carbohydrate; 1 g Dietary Fiber

Pictured on page 35.

Caramel Bananas (Philippines)

So good and yet so quick and easy.

Brown sugar, packed	2/3 cup	150 mL
Hard margarine (or butter)	3 tbsp.	50 mL
Milk	2 tbsp.	30 mL
Vanilla	1/2 tsp.	2 mL
Rum flavoring	1/2 tsp.	2 mL
Firm ripe bananas (see Tip, page 44), cut in half lengthwise, each half cut into 4 pieces	3	3
Frozen whipped topping, thawed (or ice cream)	1 cup	250 mL

(continued on next page)

Combine brown sugar, margarine and milk in small saucepan. Bring to a boil, stirring often. Reduce heat. Simmer, uncovered, for 5 minutes. Remove from heat.

Stir in vanilla and rum flavoring. Cool for 10 minutes.

Divide bananas among 4 individual serving dishes. Spoon on 2 tbsp. (30 mL) sauce per serving. Chill.

To serve, top with whipped topping. Serves 4.

1 serving: 307 Calories; 9.2 g Total Fat; 122 mg Sodium; 1 g Protein; 58 g Carbohydrate; 1 g Dietary Fiber

Tapioca Pudding (China)

Lighter than regular tapioca pudding. Serve this easy dish warm or cold.

Egg yolk (large)	1	1
Milk	1 3/4 cups	425 mL
Granulated sugar	1/3 cup	75 mL
Minute tapioca	3 tbsp.	50 mL
Salt	1/8 tsp.	0.5 mL
Can of mandarin orange segments, drained	10 oz.	284 mL
Egg white (large), room temperature	1	1
Brown sugar, packed	2 tbsp.	30 mL
Vanilla	1/2 tsp.	2 mL

Combine egg yolk and milk in heavy medium saucepan. Add granulated sugar, tapioca and salt. Heat and stir until mixture is boiling. Remove from heat.

Add orange segments. Stir.

Beat egg white in small bowl until soft peaks form. Beat in brown sugar, 1 tbsp. (15 mL) at a time. Add vanilla. Beat until stiff peaks form. Turn into medium bowl. Slowly fold orange mixture into egg white mixture. Makes 3 1/2 cups (875 mL).

1/2 cup (125 mL): 117 Calories; 1.4 g Total Fat; 87 mg Sodium; 3 g Protein; 23 g Carbohydrate; trace Dietary Fiber

Paré Pointer
Cross an eagle with a skunk and you get a bird that stinks to high heaven.

Coconut Mango Ice (Thailand)

Subtle coconut flavor comes through. This will be a big hit!

Envelopes of unflavored gelatin (1/4 oz., 7 g, each)	2	2
Water	1/2 cup	125 mL
Coconut milk	1 cup	250 mL
Granulated sugar	1 1/3 cups	325 mL
Lime juice	2 tsp.	10 mL
Chopped ripe mango (see Tip, below), about 5 medium	4 cups	1 L
Flake coconut	1/2 cup	125 mL
Whipping cream (or 1 envelope of dessert topping, prepared)	1 cup	250 mL

Sprinkle gelatin over water in large saucepan. Let stand for 1 minute. Heat and stir on medium until gelatin is dissolved.

Stir in coconut milk and sugar. Heat and stir until sugar is dissolved. Remove from heat.

Add lime juice, mango and coconut. Stir. Cool, stirring once or twice, until starting to thicken.

Whip cream in medium bowl until soft peaks form. Fold into mango mixture. Spread in shallow 12 cup (3 L) freezer container. Cover. Freeze for about 2 hours until almost firm. Process, in batches, in food processor until light and fluffy. Return to container. Cover. Freeze until solid. Makes 7 1/2 cups (1.9 L).

1/2 cup (125 mL): 209 Calories; 11 g Total Fat; 12 mg Sodium; 2 g Protein; 28 g Carbohydrate; 1 g Dietary Fiber

 To shop for ripe mangoes, look for those that yield slightly to gentle pressure. The coloring will be deep red and/or rich yellow with only a blush of green at most. Medium to large mangoes are generally the best tasting. A ripe mango will smell fairly fruity at the stem end as long as it is not cold. Avoid product that is too small, too soft or wrinkled.

Strawberry Snow (Japan)

A little snow in the tropics. Sweet, soothing and melts in the mouth.

Envelopes of unflavored gelatin (1/4 oz., 7 g, each)	2	2
Cold water	1 cup	250 mL
Granulated sugar	1 cup	250 mL
Ice cold water	1 cup	250 mL
Egg whites (large), room temperature	2	2
Lemon juice	1 tbsp.	15 mL
Fresh strawberries, trimmed and cut in half	1 lb.	454 g

Sprinkle gelatin over first amount of water in medium saucepan. Let stand for 1 minute. Heat and stir on low until gelatin is dissolved.

Stir in sugar until dissolved. Remove from heat.

Add second amount of water. Stir. Chill until thick and syrupy. Beat, with cold beaters, until frothy.

Beat egg whites in medium bowl until stiff peaks form. Beat in lemon juice. Fold gelatin mixture into egg white mixture. Turn into greased 8 × 8 inch (20 × 20 cm) pan.

Before mixture is too firm, press 1/2 of strawberries, cut side down, into bottom of pan on imaginary vertical cutting lines (1). Place remaining strawberries, cut side down, on center of each piece (2). Chill until firm. Cuts into 12 pieces.

1 piece: 86 Calories; 0.1 g Total Fat; 12 mg Sodium; 2 g Protein; 20 g Carbohydrate; 1 g Dietary Fiber

Variation: Any fruit, such as kiwifruit slices or peach slices, can be used instead of, or with, strawberries.

Pictured on page 35.

Sweet Fried Bananas (Thailand)

A traditional snack sold by vendors at Thai markets. Firm finger-sized bananas are perfect for this dish. Firm mango pieces are also delicious. Serve drizzled with Lime Ginger Sauce, page 120, or warm honey.

Rice flour	1/2 cup	125 mL
All-purpose flour	3 tbsp.	50 mL
Salt	1/2 tsp.	2 mL
Baking powder	1/4 tsp.	1 mL
Brown sugar, packed	1 tbsp.	15 mL
Medium coconut	2/3 cup	150 mL
Sesame seeds	1 tbsp.	15 mL
Milk	3/4 cup	175 mL
Finger-sized bananas (or 3 firm large bananas, cut in half lengthwise and then crosswise)	12	12
Cooking oil, for deep-frying	3 cups	750 mL

Combine first 7 ingredients in medium bowl.

Gradually stir in milk. Batter should be medium-thick consistency. Let stand for 10 minutes. Thin batter by adding milk, 1 tsp. (5 mL) at a time, to return to medium-thick consistency, if necessary.

Coat banana with batter. Deep-fry in hot (375°F, 190°C) cooking oil in large wok or deep saucepan for 3 to 4 minutes, turning several times, until golden. Remove to paper towels to drain. Makes 12 bananas.

1 banana: 130 Calories; 6.5 g Total Fat; 24 mg Sodium; 2 g Protein; 17 g Carbohydrate; 1 g Dietary Fiber

Paré Pointer
A ghost's favorite dessert is boo-berry pie topped with I-scream.

Bibimbap (Korea)

*This Veggie Beef Rice Bowl, pronounced BIH-bim-bap,
can be on the table in short order. The beef is slightly sweet
and the vegetables crisp and flavorful.*

Sirloin steak, partially frozen for easy slicing	1/2 lb.	225 g
Soy sauce	2 tbsp.	30 mL
Sesame (or cooking) oil	1 tbsp.	15 mL
Liquid honey	2 tsp.	10 mL
Sherry (or alcohol-free sherry)	2 tsp.	10 mL
Hot cooked white rice	4 cups	1 L
Cooking oil	2 tsp.	10 mL
Medium carrot, very thinly sliced	1	1
Fresh bean sprouts	1 1/2 cups	375 mL
Peeled and julienned daikon radish	1/2 cup	125 mL
Salt	1/4 tsp.	1 mL
Pepper, sprinkle		
Cayenne pepper, sprinkle		
Chopped fresh spinach leaves, packed	1 cup	250 mL

Cut steak across the grain into 1/4 x 2 inch (0.6 x 5 cm) slices. Stack, a few slices at a time, and cut lengthwise into 1/4 inch (6 mm) strips.

Combine soy sauce, sesame oil, honey and sherry in medium bowl. Add beef strips. Stir. Marinate at room temperature for 15 minutes. Heat non-stick wok or frying pan until hot. Add beef strips and marinade. Stir-fry for 2 minutes.

Place rice in 4 individual serving bowls. Divide beef mixture over rice. Keep warm.

Add next 7 ingredients to hot wok. Stir-fry for 1 minute.

Add spinach. Stir-fry for 1 minute until just wilted. Divide over beef and rice. Serves 4.

1 serving: 470 Calories; 11.5 g Total Fat; 727 mg Sodium; 19 g Protein; 71 g Carbohydrate; 2 g Dietary Fiber

Pictured on page 54.

Tender Korean Beef (Korea)

This economy-cut steak will quickly become a favorite.
So tender and succulent. Good with Rice And Clams, page 130.

Blade steak, bone-in, cut into serving-size pieces	2 1/2 lbs.	1.1 kg
Water, to cover		
Water	1/3 cup	75 mL
Soy sauce	1 tbsp.	15 mL
Sake (rice wine)	1/4 cup	60 mL
Liquid honey	2 tbsp.	30 mL
Garlic cloves, minced (or 1/2 tsp., 2 mL, powder)	2	2
Green onions, chopped	2	2
Piece of gingerroot (1 inch, 2.5 cm), peeled	1	1
Soy sauce	2 tbsp.	30 mL

Place steak in large saucepan or Dutch oven. Cover with water. Bring to a boil. Reduce heat. Cover. Simmer for 10 minutes, skimming off any foam. Drain. Rinse steak. Arrange in single layer in greased ovenproof dish.

Put next 7 ingredients into blender. Process until smooth. Pour over steak. Turn until well coated. Cover tightly with lid or foil. Bake in 250°F (120°C) oven for about 2 hours, turning once, until very tender. Strain drippings into small bowl. Skim fat from surface and discard.

Add second amount of soy sauce to drippings. Baste steak. Bake, uncovered, in 325°F (160°C) oven for about 30 minutes until juices are absorbed. Serves 5 to 6.

1 serving: 450 Calories; 29.5 g Total Fat; 743 mg Sodium; 31 g Protein; 11 g Carbohydrate; trace Dietary Fiber

1. Great Thai Salad, page 114 (Thailand)
2. Thai Dressing, page 114 (Thailand)
3. Thai Coconut Rice, page 131 (Thailand)
4. Coconut Curry Shrimp, page 87 (Thailand)

Props Courtesy Of: Artifacts
Pier 1 Imports

Asian Eggplant Stir-Fry (Vietnam)

A nice blend of ginger and lemon grass with just a hint of spice.
This is great served over noodles.

Condensed beef broth	1 cup	250 mL
Cornstarch	1 tbsp.	15 mL
Sambal oelek (chili paste)	1 tsp.	5 mL
Finely chopped lemon grass	2 tbsp.	30 mL
Oyster sauce	1 tbsp.	15 mL
Granulated sugar	1 tsp.	5 mL
Cooking oil	1 tbsp.	15 mL
Garlic cloves, minced (or 1/2 tsp., 2 mL, powder)	2	2
Minced gingerroot (or 1/4 tsp., 1 mL, ground ginger)	1 tsp.	5 mL
Sirloin steak, partially frozen for easy slicing, cut across grain into 1/8 inch (3 mm) strips	1 lb.	454 g
Cubed Asian eggplant, with peel	3 cups	750 mL
Medium red pepper, cubed	1	1
Medium yellow pepper, cubed	1	1

Combine first 6 ingredients in small bowl. Set aside.

Heat wok or frying pan until hot. Add cooking oil. Add garlic and ginger. Stir-fry for 30 seconds. Add beef strips. Stir-fry for 1 minute.

Add eggplant and both peppers. Stir-fry for 5 minutes until peppers are tender-crisp. Stir lemon grass mixture. Add to beef mixture. Heat and stir until bubbling and thickened. Makes 6 1/2 cups (1.6 L).

1 cup (250 mL): 173 Calories; 8.7 g Total Fat; 490 mg Sodium; 15 g Protein; 8 g Carbohydrate; 1 g Dietary Fiber

1. Lemon Grass Pork, page 100 (Vietnam)
2. Bibimbap (Veggie Beef Rice Bowl), page 51 (Korea)

Props Courtesy Of: Artifacts
Dansk Gifts

Chap Jae (Korea)

CHAHP-jee, Stir-Fry Beef And Noodles, has a pleasant flavor and a showy appearance. Bean threads are also called cellophane or glass noodles. They are thin, clear and a bit chewy.

Package of bean threads (or rice stick noodles), broken into small pieces	4 oz.	113 g
Boiling water, to cover		
Sesame (or cooking) oil	1 tsp.	5 mL
Lean ground beef	8 oz.	225 g
Soy sauce	1 tbsp.	15 mL
Granulated sugar	1 tsp.	5 mL
Garlic clove, minced (or 1/4 tsp., 1 mL, powder)	1	1
Green onion, sliced	1	1
Freshly ground pepper, sprinkle		
Diagonally sliced carrot	1 cup	250 mL
Sesame (or cooking) oil	4 tsp.	20 mL
Sliced fresh brown mushrooms	2 cups	500 mL
Medium onion, thinly sliced	1	1
Package of fresh baby spinach, chopped (about 3 cups, 750 mL, packed)	6 oz.	170 g
Cooking oil	1 1/2 tsp.	7 mL
Soy sauce	1 tbsp.	15 mL
Granulated sugar	2 tsp.	10 mL
Sesame seeds, toasted (see Tip, page 63), for garnish	1 tbsp.	15 mL

Cover bean threads with boiling water. Let stand for 2 minutes until softened. Drain. Set aside.

Heat wok or frying pan until hot. Add sesame oil. Add next 6 ingredients. Stir-fry for 3 to 4 minutes until no pink remains in ground beef. Transfer to large bowl.

Stir-fry carrot in 1 tsp. (5 mL) sesame oil in hot wok for 1 to 2 minutes until softened. Add to beef mixture. Repeat 3 times with remaining sesame oil, mushrooms, onion and spinach.

(continued on next page)

Heat cooking oil in hot wok until very hot. Add bean threads. Toss several times to heat through. Add beef mixture and second amounts of soy sauce and sugar. Toss several times to heat through.

Sprinkle with sesame seeds. Makes 6 cups (1.5 L). Serves 4

1 serving: 326 Calories; 13.9 g Total Fat; 601 mg Sodium; 14 g Protein; 38 g Carbohydrate; 3 g Dietary Fiber

---

Teriyaki Meatballs (Japan)

Very good flavor, not too sweet and just the right amount of tanginess.
Serve with Japan-Style Rice, page 129.

Large egg, fork-beaten	1	1
Soy sauce	1 tbsp.	15 mL
Finely chopped onion	1/4 cup	60 mL
Salt	1/2 tsp.	2 mL
Pepper	1/8 tsp.	0.5 mL
Ground ginger	1/8 tsp.	0.5 mL
Garlic powder	1/8 tsp.	0.5 mL
Fine dry bread crumbs	1/4 cup	60 mL
Lean ground beef	1 lb.	454 g
Sesame seeds, toasted (see Tip, page 63)	2 tbsp.	30 mL
SAUCE		
Water	1/4 cup	60 mL
Cornstarch	1 tbsp.	15 mL
Rice (or white) vinegar	1/4 cup	60 mL
Soy sauce	1/4 cup	60 mL
Brown sugar, packed	1/4 cup	60 mL
Ground ginger	1/4 tsp.	1 mL
Garlic powder	1/4 tsp.	1 mL

Combine first 8 ingredients in medium bowl.

Add ground beef and sesame seeds. Mix well. Shape into forty 1 inch (2.5 cm) balls. Arrange in single layer on greased baking sheet. Bake in 350°F (175°C) oven for about 15 minutes until no pink remains in meatballs.

Sauce: Stir water into cornstarch in small saucepan until smooth.

Add remaining 5 ingredients. Heat and stir until boiling and thickened. Makes 2/3 cup (150 mL) sauce. Pour over meatballs. Stir until well coated. Serves 8.

1 serving: 180 Calories; 9.4 g Total Fat; 807 mg Sodium; 12 g Protein; 12 g Carbohydrate; 1 g Dietary Fiber

Ginger Beef (China)

Good ginger flavor without the traditional deep-frying.
Great with Stir-Fried Rice, page 127.

MARINADE

Water	2 tbsp.	30 mL
Cornstarch	1 1/2 tbsp.	25 mL
Soy sauce	3 tbsp.	50 mL
White vinegar	1 1/2 tbsp.	25 mL
Granulated sugar	2 tsp.	10 mL
Sirloin steak, partially frozen for easy slicing, cut across grain into 1/8 inch (3 mm) slices	1 lb.	454 g

SAUCE

Water	1/2 cup	125 mL
Cornstarch	2 tsp.	10 mL
Beef bouillon powder	1/2 tsp.	2 mL
Seasoned salt	1/2 tsp.	2 mL
Pepper	1/8 tsp.	0.5 mL
Cooking oil	1 tbsp.	15 mL
Fresh pea pods	1 cup	250 mL
Sliced bok choy	2 cups	500 mL
Cooking oil	2 tbsp.	30 mL
Finely grated gingerroot (or 3/4 tsp., 4 mL, ground ginger)	1 tbsp.	15 mL

Marinade: Stir water into cornstarch in medium bowl until smooth.

Add soy sauce, vinegar and sugar. Stir well.

Cut beef slices into 2 inch (5 cm) strips. Add to soy sauce mixture. Stir until well coated. Marinate at room temperature for 30 minutes. Remove beef strips. Discard marinade.

Sauce: Combine first 5 ingredients in small cup until smooth.

Heat wok or frying pan until hot. Add first amount of cooking oil. Add pea pods and bok choy. Stir-fry for about 2 minutes until slightly wilted. Transfer to separate medium bowl.

(continued on next page)

Main Courses

Add second amount cooking oil to hot wok. Add beef strips and ginger. Stir-fry for about 3 minutes until beef reaches desired doneness. Add bok choy mixture. Stir sauce. Add to beef mixture. Heat and stir until boiling and thickened. Makes 3 cups (750 mL). Serves 4.

1 serving: 334 Calories; 20.7 g Total Fat; 1093 mg Sodium; 25 g Protein; 12 g Carbohydrate; 1 g Dietary Fiber

Bulgogi (Korea)

Bohl-GOH-gee, Korean Barbecued Beef, is one of the most familiar and loved recipes in Korean restaurants. Now it can be a big hit at your house. Good with Peanut Sauce, page 119, and Rice And Clams, page 130.

Garlic cloves, chopped (or 1 tsp., 5 mL, powder)	4	4
Green onions, sliced	3	3
Brown sugar, packed	3 tbsp.	50 mL
Sesame (or cooking) oil	1 tbsp.	15 mL
Sesame seeds, toasted (see Tip, page 63)	1 tbsp.	15 mL
Soy sauce	1/3 cup	75 mL
Sherry (or alcohol-free sherry)	2 tbsp.	30 mL
Cayenne pepper	1/4 tsp.	1 mL
Freshly ground pepper, sprinkle		
Beef flank steak, partially frozen for easy slicing, cut across grain into paper-thin slices	2 lbs.	900 g
Bamboo skewers, 8 inch (20 cm) length, soaked in water for 10 minutes		

Put first 9 ingredients into blender. Process until smooth.

Place beef in shallow dish or resealable freezer bag. Pour marinade over beef. Turn to coat. Cover or seal. Marinate in refrigerator for at least 2 hours to blend flavors.

Thread beef, accordion-style, onto skewers. Grill in grill pan over high heat, turning several times, until desired doneness. Serves 8.

1 serving: 250 Calories; 12.3 g Total Fat; 794 mg Sodium; 26 g Protein; 7 g Carbohydrate; trace Dietary Fiber

Pictured on page 144.

Main Courses

Beefy Spinach Noodles (China)

Has a malty flavor from the hoisin sauce. Quick and easy.

MARINADE		
Hoisin sauce	1/4 cup	60 mL
Oyster sauce	2 tbsp.	30 mL
Water	2 tbsp.	30 mL
Garlic clove, minced (or 1/4 tsp., 1 mL, powder)	1	1
Dried crushed chilies	1/4 tsp.	1 mL
Sirloin steak, partially frozen for easy slicing, cut across the grain into 1/8 inch (3 mm) slices	1 lb.	454 g
Cornstarch	1 tsp.	5 mL
Fine egg noodles	1 cup	250 mL
Boiling water	12 cups	3 L
Cooking oil (optional)	1 tbsp.	15 mL
Salt	2 tsp.	10 mL
Sesame (or cooking) oil	1 tbsp.	15 mL
Bag of spinach leaves, stems removed, thinly sliced	10 oz.	285 g
Fresh bean sprouts	1 cup	250 mL
Sliced green onion	1/4 cup	60 mL

Marinade: Combine first 5 ingredients in small cup. Stir well.

Cut beef slices into 2 inch (5 cm) strips. Place in medium bowl. Pour 1/2 of marinade over beef strips, reserving remaining marinade. Stir to coat. Marinate at room temperature for 20 minutes, stirring once. Remove beef strips, discarding marinade it was in.

Stir reserved marinade into cornstarch in small cup until smooth.

Cook noodles in boiling water, cooking oil and salt in large uncovered pot or Dutch oven for 4 to 6 minutes until tender but firm. Drain. Rinse under cold water. Set aside.

Heat wok or frying pan until hot. Add sesame oil. Add beef strips. Stir-fry for 1 to 2 minutes until half done.

(continued on next page)

Add spinach, bean sprouts and green onion. Stir. Cover. Steam for 2 to 3 minutes until spinach is wilted. Add noodles. Stir-fry to heat through. Stir cornstarch mixture. Add. Stir until boiling, thickened and glossy. Makes 5 cups (1.25 L). Serves 4.

1 serving: 402 Calories; 15.2 g Total Fat; 1400 mg Sodium; 29 g Protein; 38 g Carbohydrate; 3 g Dietary Fiber

Sukiyaki (Japan)

This is a different kind of stir-fry since there is no stirring! The vegetables are kept separate from each other and cooked in the most delicious sauce.

SAUCE		
Water	1 cup	250 mL
Beef bouillon powder	1 tsp.	5 mL
Granulated sugar	2 tbsp.	30 mL
Soy sauce	1/2 cup	125 mL
Sirloin steak, partially frozen for easy slicing, sliced paper-thin	1 lb.	454 g
Leek (white and tender parts only), cut into 2 inch (5 cm) slivers	1	1
Green onions, cut into 1 inch (2.5 cm) lengths	5	5
Can of bamboo shoots, drained	8 oz.	227 mL
Sliced suey choy (Chinese cabbage) or baby spinach leaves	2 cups	500 mL
Cooking oil	1 tsp.	5 mL

Sauce: Combine first 4 ingredients in small saucepan. Heat and stir until sugar is dissolved. Set aside.

Arrange next 5 ingredients in separate rows on platter.

Heat wok or frying pan until hot. Add cooking oil. Add beef slices. Stir-fry for 2 minutes. Remove to plate. Add vegetables individually to hot wok, arranging in wedge shape, keeping separate. Pour sauce over vegetables. Lay beef slices on top of vegetables. Cover. Reduce heat to medium. Boil for 5 minutes. Serve immediately. Serves 6.

1 serving: 185 Calories; 7.7 g Total Fat; 1613 mg Sodium; 18 g Protein; 11 g Carbohydrate; 1 g Dietary Fiber

Meatballs In Tasty Broth (Vietnam)

These tasty morsels can be served over rice or vermicelli.
A great appetizer with Peanut Sauce, page 119, or Nuoc Cham, page 121.

Small potato, peeled and diced	1	1
Inside round steak, trimmed and cut into 1 inch (2.5 cm) cubes	1 1/2 lbs.	680 g
Fish sauce	3 tbsp.	50 mL
Sesame (or cooking) oil	1 tsp.	5 mL
Granulated sugar, just a pinch		
Baking powder	1 tsp.	5 mL
Freshly ground pepper, heavy sprinkle		
Chopped fresh cilantro (optional)	2 tbsp.	30 mL
Cans of condensed beef broth (10 oz., 284 mL, each)	2	2
Water	5 1/2 cups	1.4 L
Chili sauce	3 tbsp.	50 mL
Fish sauce	1 tsp.	5 mL
Diagonally sliced green onion, for garnish	1/3 cup	75 mL
Freshly ground pepper, sprinkle		

Put potato and 1/2 of beef cubes into food processor. Pulse with on/off motion until potato is finely chopped.

Add remaining beef cubes and next 6 ingredients. Process until puréed. Traditionally, balls are formed by continually pushing and rolling 1 tbsp. (15 mL) beef mixture against your palm with thumb and fingers of same hand for about 6 times in total for each ball. This produces a very firm-textured ball that is chewy once cooked. However, the balls are very firm even if simply rolled. Makes about 50 meatballs.

Heat broth, water, chili sauce and second amount of fish sauce in large saucepan until boiling. Cook meatballs, in batches, uncovered, until meatballs are floating on surface. Time cooking for 5 minutes. Serve about 4 to 5 meatballs with about 1/4 cup (60 mL) broth.

Sprinkle with green onion and pepper.

5 meatballs with 1/4 cup (60 mL) broth: 120 Calories; 4 g Total Fat; 801 mg Sodium; 17 g Protein; 3 g Carbohydrate; trace Dietary Fiber

Variation: To make as a soup, reduce inside round steak to 1 lb. (454 g), fish sauce to 2 tbsp. (30 mL) and chopped fresh cilantro to 1 tbsp. (15 mL). Makes 36 meatballs. Each serving will have 6 meatballs and 1 cup (250 mL) broth.

Pictured on page 143.

62 Main Courses

Chicken Teriyaki (Japan)

A delicious combination of teriyaki, chicken and spinach.
Serve with Daikon Carrot Salad, page 109, and String Beans, page 132.

Soy sauce	1/4 cup	60 mL
Sake (rice wine) or sherry or fruit juice	1/4 cup	60 mL
Brown sugar, packed	3 tbsp.	50 mL
Ground ginger	1/2 tsp.	2 mL
Garlic powder	1/4 tsp.	1 mL
Dry mustard	1/8 tsp.	0.5 mL
Pepper	1/4 tsp.	1 mL
Boneless, skinless chicken breast halves (about 1 lb., 454 g)	4	4
Cooking oil	1 tbsp.	15 mL
Slivered onion	1 cup	250 mL
Frozen chopped spinach, thawed and squeezed dry	10 oz.	300 g
Sesame seeds, toasted (see Tip, below), for garnish	1 1/2 tsp.	7 mL
Green onion, thinly sliced, for garnish	1	1

Combine first 7 ingredients in medium bowl.

Add chicken. Turn until well coated. Marinate at room temperature for about 20 minutes.

Heat wok or frying pan until hot. Add cooking oil. Add onion. Stir-fry for 2 minutes. Add chicken and marinade. Cover. Simmer for 10 minutes. Turn chicken over. Simmer for 5 to 7 minutes until chicken is no longer pink.

Add spinach. Simmer until heated through.

Sprinkle with sesame seeds and green onion. Serves 4.

1 serving: 268 Calories; 6.2 g Total Fat; 1135 mg Sodium; 29 g Protein; 20 g Carbohydrate; 2 g Dietary Fiber

BEEF TERIYAKI: Omit chicken. Use same amount of a tender cut of beef, such as sirloin.

 tip

To toast nuts, coconut or sesame seeds, place in single layer in ungreased shallow pan. Bake in 350°F (175°C) oven for 5 to 10 minutes, stirring or shaking often, until desired doneness.

Meatballs With Chutney Sauce (Asia)

The sauce complements the meatballs so nicely.

Chopped onion	1/2 cup	125 mL
Garlic cloves, crushed (or	2	2
1/2 tsp., 2 mL, powder)		
Finely grated gingerroot (or	1 tsp.	5 mL
1/4 tsp., 1 mL, ground ginger)		
Cooking oil	2 tsp.	10 mL
Lean ground chicken	1 lb.	454 g
Salt	1/2 tsp.	2 mL
Cayenne pepper	1/8 tsp.	0.5 mL
Freshly ground pepper, heavy sprinkle		
Fresh bread crumbs (about 4 slices)	1 1/2 cups	375 mL
Large egg	1	1
Chopped fresh parsley (or 3 tsp.,	1/4 cup	60 mL
15 mL, flakes)		
Hoisin sauce	2 tbsp.	30 mL
CHUTNEY SAUCE		
Spicy mango (or other fruit) chutney	1 cup	250 mL
Water	1/2 cup	125 mL
Low-sodium soy sauce	1/3 cup	75 mL
Chili sauce	1 tbsp.	15 mL
Worcestershire sauce	1 tsp.	5 mL
Finely grated gingerroot (or	1 tsp.	5 mL
1/4 tsp., 1 mL, ground ginger)		

Sauté onion, garlic and ginger in cooking oil in small frying pan for 5 minutes until onion is soft and golden. Transfer to medium bowl. Cool to room temperature.

Add next 8 ingredients to onion mixture. Mix well until mixture sticks together when squeezed. Shape into 1 inch (2.5 cm) balls. Arrange in single layer on greased baking sheet. Bake on center rack in 400°F (205°C) oven for about 10 minutes until no longer pink. Remove to paper towels to drain. Makes 45 meatballs.

Chutney Sauce: Put all 6 ingredients into food processor or blender. Process until smooth. Transfer to medium saucepan. Bring to a boil, stirring constantly. Reduce heat. Simmer, uncovered, for 5 minutes. Makes 1 1/3 cups (325 mL) sauce. Pour over meatballs. Serves 6.

1 serving: 362 Calories; 14.3 g Total Fat; 1179 mg Sodium; 19 g Protein; 39 g Carbohydrate; 2 g Dietary Fiber

Pictured on page 18.

Ga-Xao-Xa-Ot (Vietnam)

Gah-joh-jah-OHT, Spicy Chicken With Lemon Grass, looks as good as it tastes.
Serve with Stir-Fry Mixed Vegetables, page 139.

MARINADE

Garlic cloves, minced (or 1/2 tsp., 2 mL, powder)	2	2
Finely grated gingerroot (or 3/4 tsp., 4 mL, ground ginger)	1 tbsp.	15 mL
Brown sugar, packed	1 tbsp.	15 mL
Sambal oelek (chili paste)	1 1/2-3 tsp.	7-15 mL
Fish sauce	2 tbsp.	30 mL
Turmeric	1/8 tsp.	0.5 mL
Stalk of lemon grass	1	1
Chicken parts, skin removed and cut into smaller pieces	3 lbs.	1.4 kg
Cooking oil	2 tbsp.	30 mL
Large onion, sliced lengthwise into wedges	1	1
Garlic cloves, minced (or 3/4 tsp., 4 mL, powder)	3	3
Chicken broth (or 1/2 tsp., 2 mL, chicken bouillon powder and 1/2 cup, 125 mL, hot water)	1/2 cup	125 mL

Marinade: Combine first 6 ingredients in large bowl. Stir well.

Remove dry straw-like pieces from lemon grass. Cut bottom 6 inches (15 cm) crosswise into very thin slices. Add to marinade. Stir.

Place chicken in shallow dish or resealable freezer bag. Pour marinade over chicken. Turn to coat. Cover or seal. Marinate in refrigerator overnight, stirring once or twice.

Heat wok or frying pan until hot. Add cooking oil. Add onion and garlic. Stir-fry for 1 minute. Add chicken with marinade. Stir-fry on high until chicken pieces are slightly browned.

Add chicken broth. Cover. Cook on medium-high for 10 minutes. Reduce heat to medium. Stir. Cook, uncovered, for 10 minutes until chicken is no longer pink and sauce is reduced. Serves 6.

1 serving: 201 Calories; 8.2 g Total Fat; 503 mg Sodium; 25 g Protein; 6 g Carbohydrate; 1 g Dietary Fiber

Thai Pizza On A Garlic Crust (Thailand)

A thin crust pizza with lots of color and crunch from the fresh vegetables.
Although not a traditional dish in Thailand, it is North America's favorite
kind of food—pizza—with a Thai kick. If you like your food spicy, add
more cayenne pepper or chili-flavored oil while cooking the chicken.
Serve with Peanut Sauce, page 119.

CRUST

All-purpose flour, approximately	1 1/3 cups	325 mL
Instant yeast	1 tsp.	5 mL
Salt	1/2 tsp.	2 mL
Garlic powder	1/4 tsp.	1 mL
Hot water	1/2 cup	125 mL
Cooking oil	1 tbsp.	15 mL
Peanut Sauce, page 119 (or commercial)	1/4 cup	60 mL
Grated part-skim mozzarella cheese	3/4 cup	175 mL
Boneless, skinless chicken breast half (about 1 large), cut into 1/8 inch (3 mm) slices	5 - 6 oz.	140 - 170 g
Medium carrot, cut julienne	1	1
Cayenne pepper	1/8 tsp.	0.5 mL
Cooking (or chili-flavored) oil	1 tbsp.	15 mL
Large red pepper, cut into 8 rings	1	1
Fresh bean sprouts, washed and blotted dry	1 cup	250 mL
Green onions, sliced diagonally	3	3
Sesame seeds, toasted (see Tip, page 63)	1 tsp.	5 mL

Crust: Food Processor Method: Measure first 4 ingredients into food
processor fitted with dough blade. With motor running, pour hot water and
first amount of cooking oil through food chute. Process for 50 to 60 seconds. If
dough seems sticky, turn out onto lightly floured surface. Knead, adding more
flour as needed, until smooth and elastic. Cover with tea towel. Let dough rest
for 15 minutes.

(continued on next page)

Hand Method: Combine first 4 ingredients in medium bowl. Add hot water and first amount of cooking oil. Mix well until dough pulls away from sides of bowl. Turn out onto lightly floured surface. Knead for 5 to 8 minutes until smooth and elastic. Cover with tea towel. Let dough rest for 15 minutes.

To Complete: Roll out and press into greased 12 inch (30 cm) pizza pan, forming rim around edge. Spread with Peanut Sauce. Sprinkle with cheese.

Sauté chicken, carrot and cayenne pepper in second amount of cooking oil in frying pan for about 5 minutes until chicken is no longer pink. Arrange over cheese.

Place red pepper around outside edge. Bake on bottom rack in 425°F (220°C) oven for 15 minutes until cheese is melted and crust is golden. Remove from oven.

Sprinkle with bean sprouts, green onion and sesame seeds. Cuts into 8 wedges.

1 wedge: 204 Calories; 8.2 g Total Fat; 359 mg Sodium; 11 g Protein; 22 g Carbohydrate; 2 g Dietary Fiber

Pictured on page 18.

Chicken And Asparagus (China)

Spicy sauce and lovely fresh taste of asparagus. Good with Spicy Radish Salad, page 112.

Water	1 cup	250 mL
Cornstarch	2 tsp.	10 mL
Chicken bouillon powder	1 tsp.	5 mL
Low-sodium soy sauce	1 tsp.	5 mL
Salt	1/4 tsp.	1 mL
Cayenne pepper	1/2 tsp.	2 mL
Fresh asparagus, cut into 1 inch (2.5 cm) pieces	3/4 lb.	340 g
Water		
Cooking oil	1 tbsp.	15 mL
Boneless, skinless chicken breast halves (about 4), cut into 3/4 inch (2 cm) cubes	1 lb.	454 g

Combine first 6 ingredients in small bowl until smooth. Set aside.

Cook asparagus in water in large saucepan until tender-crisp. Drain.

Heat wok or frying pan until hot. Add cooking oil. Add chicken. Stir-fry for 6 to 7 minutes until no longer pink. Stir cornstarch mixture. Gradually stir into chicken. Heat and stir until boiling and thickened. Sprinkle asparagus over top. Stir gently until heated through. Makes 4 cups (1 L).

1 cup (250 mL): 185 Calories; 5.7 g Total Fat; 205 mg Sodium; 28 g Protein; 5 g Carbohydrate; 1 g Dietary Fiber

Chicken Fried Noodles (Malaysia)

Has a nice hot bite. Serve with Sweet And Sour Vegetables, page 138.

Fresh chow mein noodles	1 lb.	454 g
Hot water, to cover		
Cooking oil	1 tbsp.	15 mL
Green onions, chopped	2	2
Garlic cloves, minced (or 3/4 tsp., 4 mL, powder)	3	3
Oyster sauce	2 tbsp.	30 mL
Sambal oelek (chili paste)	1 tsp.	5 mL
Curry powder	1 tsp.	5 mL
Finely chopped cooked chicken	1 cup	250 mL
Soy sauce	3 tbsp.	50 mL
Water	1/4 cup	60 mL
Fresh bean sprouts	1 cup	250 mL
Medium red pepper, slivered	1/2	1/2

Cover noodles with hot water. Let stand for 5 minutes until softened. Drain. Set aside.

Heat wok or frying pan until hot. Add cooking oil. Add green onion, garlic, oyster sauce, sambal oelek and curry powder. Stir-fry for about 1 minute until fragrant.

Add noodles, chicken, soy sauce, second amount of water, bean sprouts and red pepper. Stir-fry for about 3 minutes until heated through and noodles are coated with sauce. Makes 10 cups (2.5 L).

1 cup (250 mL): 149 Calories; 4.5 g Total Fat; 672 mg Sodium; 12 g Protein; 14 g Carbohydrate; 1 g Dietary Fiber

Pictured on page 90.

Punjab Chicken (India)

Also known as Tandoori Chicken. Serve with Indian Side Salad, page 34, or Cucumber Raita, page 38, to cool the palate.

Bone-in chicken breasts, legs, and thighs (about 16 pieces), skin removed	3 1/2 lbs.	1.6 kg

(continued on next page)

Garlic cloves (or 1 1/2 tsp., 7 mL, powder)	6	6
Coarsely chopped onion	2 cups	500 mL
Piece of gingerroot (1 inch, 2.5 cm), peeled (or 1/4 tsp., 1 mL, ground ginger)	1	1
Chopped fresh cilantro, packed	1/4 cup	60 mL
Fresh small red chilies (seeds and ribs removed for less heat, see Tip, page 121)	2	2
Salt	1 tsp.	5 mL
Paprika	2 tsp.	10 mL
Garam Masala, page 40 (or commercial)	1 tsp.	5 mL
Turmeric	1/2 tsp.	2 mL
Black mustard seed	2 tsp.	10 mL
Cumin seed	2 tsp.	10 mL
Whole green cardamom	10	10
Freshly grated lemon zest	4 tsp.	20 mL
Freshly squeezed lemon juice (about 1 small)	3 tbsp.	50 mL
Plain yogurt	2 cups	500 mL

Cut chicken breasts in half. Cut 2 or 3 deep slashes through fleshiest portion of each half. Place chicken in large non-metal bowl.

Put next 9 ingredients into food processor. Process until finely chopped.

Heat and stir mustard seed, cumin seed and cardamom in frying pan on medium-high for about 1 minute until mustard seed starts to pop and spices become fragrant. Add to onion mixture.

Add lemon zest, lemon juice and yogurt. Process until almost smooth. Pour over chicken. Stir to coat. Cover. Chill for 12 to 24 hours, stirring a few times to keep chicken well coated. Remove chicken from marinade leaving as much on chicken as possible. Discard excess marinade. Place chicken on greased foil-lined baking sheet. Broil for about 10 minutes until golden. Bake, uncovered, on center rack in 350°F (175°C) oven for about 40 minutes until no longer pink. Coating should be slightly dried. Makes about 16 pieces.

1 piece: 151 Calories; 3.9 g Total Fat; 174 mg Sodium; 22 g Protein; 7 g Carbohydrate; 1 g Dietary Fiber

Pictured on page 126.

Variation: Grill chicken over high heat on greased grill, turning several times, until slightly charred and brown in places. Turn off one element. Cook chicken, using indirect method, for about 20 minutes until no longer pink.

Coco-Milk Chicken (Indonesia)

This Indonesian dish has a smooth exceptional taste. Serve over rice.
Or try with Green Bean Stir-Fry, page 132, or Nasi Goreng, page 134.

Whole chicken, skin removed and cut into serving-size pieces	3 lbs.	1.4 kg
Cooking oil	2 tbsp.	30 mL
Garlic cloves, minced (or 3/4 tsp., 4 mL, powder)	3	3
Minced gingerroot (or 3/4 tsp., 4 mL, ground ginger)	1 tbsp.	15 mL
Medium onion, thinly sliced	1	1
Fresh small red chili (seeds and ribs removed for less heat), minced (see Tip, page 121)	1	1
Ground coriander	3/4 tsp.	4 mL
Coconut milk	2 cups	500 mL
Salt	1/2 tsp.	2 mL
Pepper (white is best)	1/4 tsp.	1 mL
Cashews, coarsely chopped	1/2 cup	125 mL

Fry chicken in cooking oil in frying pan for about 20 minutes, turning over once, until golden. Transfer to large plate. Cover. Keep warm.

Sauté next 5 ingredients in same frying pan for about 3 minutes until onion is soft and starting to turn golden.

Add coconut milk, salt and pepper. Stir. Simmer, uncovered, for 10 minutes. Add chicken. Cover. Simmer for about 45 minutes, turning chicken over once, until tender and no longer pink.

Sprinkle with cashews. Serves 4.

1 serving: 616 Calories; 46 g Total Fat; 443 mg Sodium; 41 g Protein; 14 g Carbohydrate; 1 g Dietary Fiber

1. Peppered Chicken, page 73 (China)
2. East Indian Coconut Rice, page 128 (India)
3. Green Bean Stir-Fry, page 132 (Indonesia)

Props Courtesy Of: Pier 1 Imports
Winners Stores

Peppered Chicken (China)

Brightly colored. Nicely flavored. Great with either
Nutty Steamed Rice, page 129, or Orange-Flavored Rice, page 130.

Water	1 tbsp.	15 mL
Cornstarch	2 tsp.	10 mL
Soy sauce	2 tsp.	10 mL
Salt	3/4 tsp.	4 mL
Pepper	1/8 tsp.	0.5 mL
Boneless, skinless chicken breast halves (about 4), cut into 1/2 inch (12 mm) cubes	1 lb.	454 g
Cooking oil	1 tbsp.	15 mL
Medium green pepper, cut into 1/2 inch (12 mm) chunks	1	1
Medium red pepper, cut into 1/2 inch (12 mm) chunks	1	1
Soy sauce	1 tbsp.	15 mL
Sherry (or alcohol-free sherry) or prepared orange juice	2 tbsp.	30 mL
Dried crushed chilies (optional)	1/4 tsp.	1 mL

Combine first 5 ingredients in medium bowl until smooth. Add chicken. Let stand for 15 minutes.

Heat wok or frying pan until hot. Add cooking oil. Add both peppers and chicken mixture. Stir-fry for 7 minutes.

Add second amount of soy sauce, sherry and chilies. Stir-fry for 2 to 3 minutes until chicken is no longer pink. Makes 4 cups (1 L).

1 cup (250 mL): 194 Calories; 5.5 g Total Fat; 882 mg Sodium; 27 g Protein; 7 g Carbohydrate; 1 g Dietary Fiber

Pictured on page 71.

1. Banh Pho Bo (Beef Noodle Soup), page 140 (Vietnam)
2. Kung-Pao Chicken, page 76 (China)

Main Courses

Chicken Curry Wraps (India)

Delicate curry with a sweet raisin surprise. Use hot curry paste if you like more heat. Serve with Indian Side Salad, page 34.

Sliced onion	1 cup	250 mL
Cooking oil	1 tbsp.	15 mL
Boneless, skinless chicken breast halves (about 2), diced	8 oz.	225 g
Garlic clove, minced (or 1/4 tsp., 1 mL, powder)	1	1
Finely grated gingerroot (or 1/8 tsp., 0.5 mL, ground ginger)	1/2 tsp.	2 mL
Mild curry paste	1 tbsp.	15 mL
Jalapeño pepper, seeded and finely chopped (see Note)	1	1
Medium green pepper, diced	1	1
Fresh okra (or frozen, thawed), sliced 1/2 inch (12 mm) thick	5	5
Medium tomato, diced	1	1
Dark raisins	2 tbsp.	30 mL
Plain yogurt	2 tbsp.	30 mL
Cooked short grain rice	4 cups	1 L
Whole wheat flour tortillas (10 inch, 25 cm, size)	8	8
Diced cucumber	2 cups	500 mL
Shredded iceberg lettuce	2 2/3 cups	650 mL
Plain yogurt	1 cup	250 mL

Cook onion in cooking oil in large frying pan for about 5 minutes until soft.

Add chicken, garlic and ginger. Heat and stir for 3 minutes.

Add next 6 ingredients. Stir. Cover. Simmer for 15 to 20 minutes, stirring occasionally, until chicken is no longer pink and vegetables are tender.

Stir in first amount of yogurt. Remove from heat. Makes 2 2/3 cups (650 mL) filling.

Place 1/2 cup (125 mL) rice in center of each tortilla. Press down slightly. Spoon about 1/3 cup (75 mL) filling over rice.

Top with cucumber, lettuce and yogurt. Roll tortilla around filling, tucking in sides and pressing slightly to enclose tightly. To serve, cut in half at sharp angle. Makes 16 halves.

(continued on next page)

1 half: 212 Calories; 2.8 g Total Fat; 186 mg Sodium; 9 g Protein; 39 g Carbohydrate; 3 g Dietary Fiber

Note: Wear gloves when chopping jalapeño peppers and avoid touching your eyes.

Spinach Chicken Teriyaki (Japan)

Mild teriyaki flavor with a touch of ginger. Great presentation!
Serve with Japan-Style Rice, page 129.

MARINADE		
Mirin (Japanese sweet cooking seasoning)	1/2 cup	125 mL
Sake (rice wine)	1/2 cup	125 mL
Soy sauce	1/2 cup	125 mL
Water	1/4 cup	60 mL
Finely grated gingerroot (or 3/4 tsp., 4 mL, ground ginger)	1 tbsp.	15 mL
Garlic clove, minced (or 1/4 tsp., 1 mL, powder)	1	1
Boneless, skinless chicken breast halves (about 1 1/2 lbs., 680 g)	6	6
TOPPING		
Frozen chopped spinach, thawed and squeezed dry	10 oz.	300 g
Mayonnaise	3 tbsp.	50 mL
Miso (fermented soybean paste)	1 tbsp.	15 mL
Sake (rice wine)	2 tsp.	10 mL
Granulated sugar	2 tsp.	10 mL

Marinade: Combine first 6 ingredients in medium bowl.

Place chicken in shallow dish or resealable freezer bag. Pour marinade over chicken. Turn to coat. Cover or seal. Marinate in refrigerator for 30 to 60 minutes, turning 2 or 3 times. Remove chicken. Discard marinade. Arrange chicken in single layer on greased baking sheet, fleshy side up. Bake in 350°F (175°C) oven for 20 minutes. Chicken will be partially cooked.

Topping: Mash all 5 ingredients together in small bowl. Spread over chicken, making sure to cover each piece. Bake for about 10 minutes until no pink remains in chicken. Serves 6.

1 serving: 283 Calories; 7.8 g Total Fat; 1626 mg Sodium; 29 g Protein; 12 g Carbohydrate; 1 g Dietary Fiber

Pictured on page 126.

Kung-Pao Chicken (China)

This recipe has a very delicate heat. More chilies or chili paste can be added if you like it fire-alarm hot! Sauce has a great flavor. Serve over noodles.

SAUCE

Water	2 tbsp.	30 mL
Hoisin sauce	1 tbsp.	15 mL
Soy sauce	1 tbsp.	15 mL
Sambal oelek (chili paste)	1/2 - 1 tsp.	2 - 5 mL
Cornstarch	1 tbsp.	15 mL
Soy sauce	1 tbsp.	15 mL
Cornstarch	1 tbsp.	15 mL
Boneless, skinless chicken breast halves and thighs, diced	1 lb.	454 g
Sesame (or cooking) oil	1 tsp.	5 mL
Egg white (large), fork-beaten	1	1
Garlic clove, crushed (or 1/4 tsp., 1 mL, powder)	1	1
Cooking oil	1 tbsp.	15 mL
Garlic clove, crushed (or 1/4 tsp., 1 mL, powder)	1	1
Finely grated gingerroot (or 1/8 tsp., 0.5 mL, ground ginger)	1/2 tsp.	2 mL
Small carrots, thinly sliced on sharp diagonal	2	2
Medium green pepper, diced	1/2	1/2
Medium red pepper, diced	1/2	1/2
Fresh small red chilies (seeds and ribs removed for less heat, see Tip, page 121), optional	1 - 5	1 - 5
Green onions, cut on diagonal into 1 inch (2.5 cm) pieces	3	3
Cooking oil	1 tbsp.	15 mL

Sauce: Stir first 5 ingredients in small cup until smooth. Set aside.

Stir second amount of soy sauce into second amount of cornstarch in medium bowl until smooth.

Add chicken, sesame oil, egg white and garlic. Mix until chicken is very well coated.

(continued on next page)

Heat wok or frying pan until hot. Add cooking oil. Add garlic, ginger and carrot. Stir-fry for 1 minute.

Add next 4 ingredients. Stir-fry for 1 to 2 minutes until peppers are tender-crisp. Transfer to medium bowl.

Add second amount of cooking oil to hot wok. Add chicken mixture. Stir immediately to break up chicken pieces. Stir-fry on medium-high for about 3 minutes until chicken is no longer pink. Stir sauce. Stir into chicken mixture until boiling and thickened. Add pepper mixture. Heat and stir until peppers are coated and mixture is heated through. Makes 4 cups (1 L).

1 cup (250 mL): 292 Calories; 12.5 g Total Fat; 711 mg Sodium; 29 g Protein; 16 g Carbohydrate; 2 g Dietary Fiber

Pictured on page 72.

Honey Ginger Chicken (Vietnam)

Dark, glistening and tasty. Serve with Stir-Fry Mixed Vegetables, page 139.

Cooking oil	2 tbsp.	30 mL
Large onion, cut into wedges	1	1
Chicken thighs, skin removed	2 lbs.	900 g
Garlic cloves, thinly sliced (or 1 tsp., 5 mL, powder)	4	4
Piece of gingerroot (1 inch, 2.5 cm), peeled and finely grated	1	1
Water	1/2 cup	125 mL
Liquid honey	1/4 cup	60 mL
Fish sauce	1 tbsp.	15 mL
Soy sauce	2 tbsp.	30 mL
Oyster sauce	2 tbsp.	30 mL
Pepper	1/8 tsp.	0.5 mL

Heat wok or frying pan until hot. Add cooking oil. Add onion. Stir-fry for 5 to 7 minutes until onion is soft and golden.

Add chicken. Cook for about 10 minutes until all sides are browned.

Add garlic and ginger. Heat and stir until fragrant.

Combine remaining 6 ingredients in small bowl. Add to chicken mixture. Stir until well coated. Reduce heat to medium. Cook for about 20 minutes until no pink remains in chicken. Serves 4.

1 serving: 358 Calories; 14.4 g Total Fat; 1422 mg Sodium; 28 g Protein; 30 g Carbohydrate; 1 g Dietary Fiber

Pictured on page 126.

Chicken Yakitori (Japan)

Yah-kee-TOH-ree is a beautiful kabob with a bit of sweetness and a wee bit of nip. Serve with Cabbage Fry, page 136, or Spiffy Carrots, page 136.

SAUCE		
Sake (rice wine) or sherry (or alcohol-free sherry)	1/3 cup	75 mL
Soy sauce	1/3 cup	75 mL
Granulated sugar	2 tbsp.	30 mL
Garlic powder	1/8 tsp.	0.5 mL
Cayenne pepper	1/4 tsp.	1 mL
Small red pepper, cut into about twelve 1 inch (2.5 cm) squares	1	1
Boneless, skinless chicken breast halves (about 4), cut into about twenty-four 1 1/2 inch (3.8 cm) cubes	1 lb.	454 g
Small green pepper, cut into about twelve 1 inch (2.5 cm) squares	1	1
Fresh whole mushrooms, stems removed	12	12
Leek (white and tender parts only), cut into 1 inch (2.5 cm) lengths	1	1
Metal skewers, 12 inch (30 cm) length	6	6
Underripe cherry tomatoes	6	6

Sauce: Mix first 5 ingredients in small saucepan. Bring to a boil, stirring occasionally.

Thread next 5 ingredients onto skewers ending with 1 tomato per skewer. Place on greased grill over medium-high heat. Brush with sauce. Cook for 4 to 5 minutes per side, brushing with sauce several times. Makes 6 kabobs.

1 kabob: 170 Calories; 1.6 g Total Fat; 972 mg Sodium; 20 g Protein; 15 g Carbohydrate; 2 g Dietary Fiber

Pictured on front cover.

BEEF YAKITORI: Omit chicken. Use same amount of a tender cut of beef, such as sirloin.

Chicken And Pork Stew (Philippines)

Some call it soup. Some call it stew. Whatever you call it, this wonderful dish can be as thick or as thin as you like according to how much cornstarch you add. Serve with Cassava Biscuits, page 124.

Boneless, skinless chicken breast halves (about 3), cut bite size	3/4 lb.	340 g
Boneless pork loin, cut bite size	3/4 lb.	340 g
Medium onion, chopped	1	1
Cooking oil	1 tbsp.	15 mL
Can of diced tomatoes, with juice	14 oz.	398 mL
Medium green pepper, chopped	1	1
Water	3 cups	750 mL
Chicken bouillon powder	1 tbsp.	15 mL
Dried whole oregano	1/2 tsp.	2 mL
Salt	1 tsp.	5 mL
Pepper	1/2 tsp.	2 mL
Medium potatoes, cut bite size	3	3
Water	3 tbsp.	50 mL
Cornstarch	3 - 5 tbsp.	50 - 75 mL

Brown chicken, pork and onion, in 2 batches, in cooking oil in frying pan. Turn into large pot or Dutch oven.

Add next 7 ingredients. Stir. Bring to a boil. Cover. Reduce heat. Simmer for 45 to 60 minutes until chicken and pork are tender.

Add potato. Cook for 20 to 25 minutes until tender.

Stir second amount of water into cornstarch in small cup until smooth. Stir into stew until boiling and thickened. Makes 8 1/2 cups (2.1 L).

1 cup (250 mL): 199 Calories; 7 g Total Fat; 607 mg Sodium; 19 g Protein; 15 g Carbohydrate; 2 g Dietary Fiber

Paré Pointer

Johnny argued that two times ten equals two times eleven. Two times ten is twenty. Two times eleven is twenty too.

Rolled Sole In Coconut Sauce
(Vietnam)

A hint of ginger in this rich sauce makes the taste extra special. A wonderful dish to impress dinner guests. "North Americanized" in the use of fillets instead of whole fish. Serve with rice or noodles or Spicy Radish Salad, page 112.

Finely chopped gingerroot (or 3/4 tsp., 4 mL, ground ginger)	1 tbsp.	15 mL
Salt	1/2 tsp.	2 mL
Brown sugar, packed	1 tbsp.	15 mL
Freshly ground pepper, sprinkle		
Sole fillets (about 1 1/2 lbs., 680 g)	6	6
COCONUT SAUCE		
Oyster sauce	1 tbsp.	15 mL
Coconut milk	2 tbsp.	30 mL
Sambal oelek (chili paste), optional	1/2 tsp.	2 mL
Cooking oil	3 tbsp.	50 mL
Large onion, halved lengthwise and thinly sliced	1	1
Garlic cloves, minced (or 3/4 tsp., 4 mL, powder)	3	3
Dried shiitake mushrooms	4	4
Hot water	2 cups	500 mL
Coconut milk	6 tbsp.	100 mL
Finely chopped roasted peanuts, for garnish	2 tbsp.	30 mL

Combine ginger, salt, brown sugar and pepper in small bowl.

Lay fillets flat on work surface. Sprinkle ginger mixture over fillets. Pat lightly onto surface. Gently roll fillets from narrowest end. Arrange seam side down and slightly apart from one another in ungreased shallow casserole. Casserole should fit on rack in wok or large saucepan.

Coconut Sauce: Combine oyster sauce, first amount of coconut milk and sambal oelek in small cup. Pour over rolls.

Heat wok or frying pan until hot. Add cooking oil. Add onion and garlic. Stir-fry for about 5 minutes until onion is starting to turn golden. Spoon over rolls.

(continued on next page)

Soak mushrooms in hot water for 10 minutes. Drain. Discard tough mushroom stems. Thinly slice mushrooms. Scatter over rolls. Place casserole on rack about 1 inch (2.5 cm) over boiling water in wok or large saucepan. Cover. Let steam build up for about 2 minutes. Reduce heat to medium. Cook for about 12 minutes until fish is opaque. Remove rolls to serving dish.

Stir second amount of coconut milk into liquid in casserole. Drizzle over rolls.

Sprinkle with peanuts. Serve immediately. Serves 6.

1 serving: 234 Calories; 12.5 g Total Fat; 506 mg Sodium; 22 g Protein; 8 g Carbohydrate; 1 g Dietary Fiber

---

Cooked Whole Trout (Indonesia)

You may prefer this with the "head off in the kitchen." Has a very slight taste of coconut. Serve with Green Bean Stir-Fry, page 132 or Nasi Goreng, page 134.

Whole trout fish, pan ready	1 1/2 lbs.	680 g
Lime juice	2 tbsp.	30 mL
Salt	1 tsp.	5 mL
Piece of gingerroot (1/4 inch, 6 mm), peeled	1	1
Garlic cloves, coarsely chopped (or 3/4 tsp., 4 mL, powder)	3	3
Lemon grass, bulb only (root and stalk removed)	1	1
Small fresh red chili	1	1
Shallots	2	2
Coconut milk	1 cup	250 mL
Turmeric	1/4 tsp.	1 mL
Granulated sugar	1 tsp.	5 mL
Cashews	1/4 cup	60 mL

Make several slashes on fish being careful not to cut through backbone. Rub inside and outside of fish with lime juice and salt.

Put remaining 9 ingredients into food processor or blender. Process until smooth. Coat fish. Place on greased broiler pan. Broil for 8 minutes. Turn fish over. Brush with coconut mixture. Broil for 7 to 8 minutes until fish flakes easily when tested with fork. Serves 4 to 5.

1 serving: 423 Calories; 26.2 g Total Fat; 664 mg Sodium; 39 g Protein; 9 g Carbohydrate; 1 g Dietary Fiber

Sauced Halibut (India)

An excellent dish with mild curry taste and a bit of tang.
Good with East Indian Coconut Rice, page 128.

Chopped onion	1 1/2 cups	375 mL
Garlic cloves, minced (or 1/2 tsp., 2 mL, powder)	2	2
Finely grated gingerroot (or 1/2 tsp., 2 mL, ground ginger)	2 tsp.	10 mL
Cooking oil	2 tbsp.	30 mL
Curry paste	2 tsp.	10 mL
Can of diced tomatoes, with juice	14 oz.	398 mL
Medium apple, peeled and diced (about 1 cup, 250 mL)	1	1
Whole cardamom, bruised (see Tip, page 41)	6	6
Plain yogurt	1/2 cup	125 mL
All-purpose flour	2 tsp.	10 mL
Halibut fillet, fresh or frozen, thawed, cut into 1 1/2 inch (3.8 cm) cubes	1 lb.	454 g

Sauté onion, garlic and ginger in cooking oil in large saucepan on medium for about 10 minutes, stirring frequently, until onion is very soft.

Add curry paste. Heat and stir for 1 minute until fragrant. Add tomatoes with juice, apple and cardamom. Stir. Reduce heat. Cover. Simmer for 25 minutes until apple is very soft. Remove and discard cardamom.

Stir yogurt into flour in small dish until smooth. Stir into curry mixture until boiling.

Gently stir fish into curry mixture. Cover. Cook on medium for 8 to 10 minutes until fish flakes easily when tested with fork and sauce is boiling and thickened. Makes 4 cups (1 L).

1 cup (250 mL): 296 Calories; 11.5 g Total Fat; 252 mg Sodium; 28 g Protein; 21 g Carbohydrate; 3 g Dietary Fiber

 tip *To shop for fresh fish, look for protruding, bright, clear eyes and pink or red gills. A stale fish will have sunken, cloudy, pink eyes and gray gills.*

Somen And Fish (Japan)

Flaky fillets of fish with tender SOH-mehn noodles and a smoky fish sauce.
Serve with Japan-Style Rice, page 129.

Water	2/3 cup	150 mL
Soy sauce	1/4 cup	60 mL
Dashi (fish stock)	1/4 tsp.	1 mL
Onion powder	1/4 tsp.	1 mL
Snapper (or other) fillets	1 1/2 lbs.	680 g
Salt, sprinkle		
Package of somen noodles	14 oz.	400 g
Boiling water	8 cups	2 L
Salt	3/4 tsp.	4 mL
Chopped green onion, for garnish	1 tbsp.	15 mL

Combine first 4 ingredients in large saucepan. Bring to a boil.

Add fillets and salt. Reduce heat. Cover. Simmer for about 10 minutes until fillets flake easily when tested with fork.

Cook noodles in boiling water and salt in large uncovered pot or Dutch oven for 2 to 3 minutes until tender but firm. Drain. Transfer to warm platter. Gently remove fillets from saucepan. Arrange over noodles. Pour sauce over fillets and noodles.

Garnish with green onion. Serves 6.

1 serving: 360 Calories; 2.1 g Total Fat; 2058 mg Sodium; 32 g Protein; 51 g Carbohydrate; 3 g Dietary Fiber

 To help remove odors from handling fish, rub your hands thoroughly with salt or vinegar. Rinse.

Tea-Poached Halibut (Vietnam)

An absolutely wonderful cold dish. The tea gives a unique soft flavor and a beige color. This fish is delicious in a lettuce leaf wrapper or on its own as a lunch or first course. Or try serving with Stir-Fry Mixed Vegetables, page 139.

Water	4 cups	1 L
Oyster sauce	1/4 cup	60 mL
Orange pekoe tea bags	2	2
Finely grated gingerroot (or	1 tsp.	5 mL
1/4 tsp., 1 mL, ground ginger)		
Liquid honey	1 tbsp.	15 mL
Halibut fillets, fresh or frozen,	1 1/2 lbs.	680 g
thawed, visible pin bones removed		

Combine first 5 ingredients in large frying pan. Bring to a boil.

Carefully add fillets to sauce. Simmer, uncovered, for 1 hour. Turn fillets over. Remove and discard tea bags. Cook, uncovered, for 30 minutes until sauce is reduced to 3/4 cup (175 mL). Cover. Cool to room temperature. Remove and discard skin. Serve at room temperature or chilled, drizzled with sauce. Serves 4.

1 serving: 224 Calories; 4 g Total Fat; 1372 mg Sodium; 36 g Protein; 9 g Carbohydrate; trace Dietary Fiber

 To freshen the flavor of frozen fish, thaw covered completely in milk. Discard milk.

Coconut Cabbage With Fish (Malaysia)

Deep golden and coral color. Just the right sauciness. Very different but tasty because of the cabbage and fish combination.

Chopped shallots	1/2 cup	125 mL
Curry paste	2 tsp.	10 mL
Small green pepper, slivered	1	1
Small red pepper, slivered	1	1
Cooking oil	2 tsp.	10 mL
Coconut milk	1 cup	250 mL
Granulated sugar	2 tbsp.	30 mL
Freshly squeezed lime juice	1 tbsp.	15 mL
Finely chopped gingerroot (or 3/4 tsp., 4 mL, ground ginger)	1 tbsp.	15 mL
Garlic cloves, minced (or 1/2 tsp., 2 mL, powder)	2	2
Vegetable cocktail juice	1 cup	250 mL
Halibut fillets, fresh or frozen, thawed, skin removed and cut into 1 inch (2.5 cm) cubes	1 lb.	454 g
Thinly shredded cabbage	4 cups	1 L

Sauté shallots, curry paste and both peppers in cooking oil in wok or frying pan on medium-high for 4 minutes.

Add next 6 ingredients. Bring to a boil. Reduce heat. Simmer, uncovered, for 4 minutes.

Add fish. Cover. Cook for 4 minutes.

Arrange cabbage over fish. Cover. Cook for 4 minutes until fish flakes easily when tested with fork. Makes 4 3/4 cups (1.2 L). Serves 4.

1 serving: 358 Calories; 18.9 g Total Fat; 320 mg Sodium; 27 g Protein; 23 g Carbohydrate; 3 g Dietary Fiber

 To store fish, wrap loosely and keep in refrigerator. Cook within 24 hours of purchase. Fish wrapped and stored in the freezer will keep for 2 to 3 months.

Shrimp Mango Curry (Malaysia)

Rich, golden yellow sauce. Delicate curry flavor with slight chili bite. Serve over rice.

Ripe medium mango, peeled and chopped (see Tip, page 48)	1	1
Chopped onion	1/2 cup	125 mL
Diced celery	3/4 cup	175 mL
Garlic clove, minced (or 1/4 tsp., 1 mL, powder)	1	1
Hard margarine (or butter)	1 tbsp.	15 mL
All-purpose flour	3 tbsp.	50 mL
Curry paste	1 1/2 tsp.	7 mL
Sambal oelek (chili paste)	1 tsp.	5 mL
Coconut milk	1 1/3 cups	325 mL
Dark raisins	1/2 cup	125 mL
Chicken broth	2 cups	500 mL
Raw large shrimp, peeled and deveined, tails intact (see Tip, below)	1 1/2 lbs.	680 g
Salt	1/4 tsp.	1 mL
Brown sugar, packed	1 tbsp.	15 mL

Sauté mango, onion, celery and garlic in margarine in wok or frying pan on medium-high for 5 minutes until onion is golden.

Add flour, curry paste and sambal oelek. Stir. Cook for 1 minute, stirring frequently.

Gradually add coconut milk, raisins and broth, stirring constantly, until boiling. Reduce heat. Simmer, uncovered, for 5 minutes.

Add shrimp, salt and brown sugar. Stir. Cook for 3 minutes until shrimp turns pink and is curled. Makes about 7 cups (1.75 L).

1 cup (250 mL): 310 Calories; 14.4 g Total Fat; 504 mg Sodium; 23 g Protein; 24 g Carbohydrate; 2 g Dietary Fiber

Pictured on page 36.

tip *To devein shrimp or prawns, strip off legs and peel off shell, leaving tail intact, if desired. Using a small, sharp knife, make a shallow cut along the center of the back. Rinse under cold water to wash out the dark vein. To devein shrimp that you want to cook in the shell, simply slit along back right through the shell to remove the vein.*

Coconut Curry Shrimp (Thailand)

Serve over basmati or jasmine rice with a squeeze of lime juice and chopped fresh coriander leaves. The sauce can be prepared well ahead and refrigerated.

SAUCE		
Can of coconut milk	14 oz.	400 mL
Fish sauce	2 tbsp.	30 mL
Sesame (or cooking) oil	2 tsp.	10 mL
Thai red curry paste	2 tsp.	10 mL
Raw large shrimp, peeled and deveined, tails intact (see Tip, page 86)	1 lb.	454 g
Medium red pepper, slivered	1	1
Fresh pea pods (about 3 oz., 85 g), cut in half diagonally	1 cup	250 mL
Green onions, sliced	3	3

Sauce: Combine first 4 ingredients in large heavy saucepan. Bring to a boil on medium-high, stirring constantly. Reduce heat to medium. Boil for 15 to 20 minutes, stirring frequently, until sauce is thickened and reduced to about 1 cup (250 mL).

Butterfly shrimp by cutting slightly deeper in cut made for deveining, but not quite through. Press open. Pat dry. Add to sauce.

Add red pepper, pea pods and green onion. Heat and stir for about 3 minutes until shrimp turns pink, is curled and completely coated with sauce. Do not overcook. Makes 4 1/3 cups (1.1 L). Serves 4.

1 serving: 373 Calories; 25.6 g Total Fat; 706 mg Sodium; 27 g Protein; 11 g Carbohydrate; 2 g Dietary Fiber

Pictured on page 53 and back cover.

 To thaw frozen shrimp safely and quickly, place in colander under cold running water. Do not refreeze.

Sake Fish (Japan)

Wonderful SAH-kee and soy flavor. Fish is moist and flaky.
Serve with String Beans, page 132, or Spiffy Carrots, page 136.

Soy sauce	1/3 cup	75 mL
Sake (rice wine)	1/4 cup	60 mL
Water	1/2 cup	125 mL
Granulated sugar	2 tbsp.	30 mL
Snapper (or other) fillets (about 1 lb., 454 g)	4	4

Measure soy sauce, sake, water and sugar into frying pan. Stir. Bring to a gentle boil.

Add fillets. Cover. Simmer for about 10 minutes, turning over once, until fillets flake easily when tested with fork. Serves 4.

1 serving: 217 Calories; 6.7 g Total Fat; 1504 mg Sodium; 24 g Protein; 10 g Carbohydrate; 0 g Dietary Fiber

Pictured on page 89.

SAKE OVEN FISH: Pour sauce into shallow baking pan large enough to hold fillets in single layer. Add fillets. Bake in 350°F (175°C) oven for 8 minutes. Turn over. Bake for 7 to 8 minutes, basting often, until fillets flake easily when tested with fork.

1. Sake Fish, this page (Japan)
2. Lemon Petal, page 11
3. Daikon Carrot Salad, page 109 (Japan)
4. Japanese Primavera, page 104 (Japan)

Props Courtesy Of: Artifacts
Dansk Gifts
Winners Stores

Seafood Dim Sum (China)

Dim Sum is Cantonese for "heart's delight." Serve these little dumplings
with a dipping sauce for your heart's delight.

Raw medium shrimp, peeled, deveined (see Tip, page 86) and finely chopped	3/4 lb.	340 g
Scallops, finely chopped	6 oz.	170 g
Finely chopped onion	3 tbsp.	50 mL
Sherry (or alcohol-free sherry), optional	1 tbsp.	15 mL
Finely grated gingerroot (or 1/4 tsp., 1 mL, ground ginger)	1 tsp.	5 mL
Sake (rice wine)	1 tbsp.	15 mL
Soy sauce	1 tbsp.	15 mL
Round dumpling wrappers	40	40

Combine first 7 ingredients in medium bowl. Makes 2 2/3 cups (650 mL) filling.

Put 1 tbsp. (15 mL) filling in center of each wrapper. Gather edges up to center. Spray 9 inch (22 cm) bamboo steamer well with cooking spray. Place bamboo steamer in large wok over simmering water. Arrange 10 dumplings, not touching each other or sides of steamer, in steamer. Cover. Steam for 15 minutes. Repeat until all dumplings are cooked. Makes 40 dumplings.

1 dumpling: 37 Calories; 0.3 g Total Fat; 91 mg Sodium; 3 g Protein; 5 g Carbohydrate;
trace Dietary Fiber

Pictured on page 125.

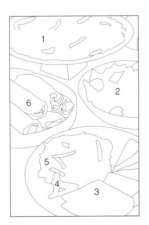

1. Chicken Fried Noodles, page 68 (Malaysia)
2. Pork And Peppers, page 93 (Japan)
3. Mandarin Pancakes, page 122 (China)
4. Pepper Triangle, page 11
5. Moo Shu Pork, page 92 (China)
6. Moo Shu Pork, page 92, with Mandarin Pancakes, page 122 (China)

Props Courtesy Of: Artifacts
                  Pier 1 Imports
                  Stokes
                  X/S Wares

Moo Shu Pork (China)

MOO-shoo is a stir-fry dish with pork and eggs rolled in small, thin pancakes. Ginger and garlic flavors throughout.

MARINADE
Water	1 tbsp.	15 mL
Cornstarch	1 tbsp.	15 mL
Soy sauce	1 1/2 tbsp.	25 mL
Granulated sugar	1/2 tsp.	2 mL
Sherry or sake (rice wine)	1 tbsp.	15 mL
Pepper	1/8 tsp.	0.5 mL
Pork tenderloin (or pork loin), cut into 1/4 inch (6 mm) strips	3/4 lb.	340 g
Dried shiitake mushrooms	3	3
Boiling water, to cover		
Large eggs	3	3
Salt	1/2 tsp.	2 mL
Pepper	1/16 tsp.	0.5 mL
Cooking oil	1 tbsp.	15 mL
Shredded suey choy (Chinese cabbage)	2 cups	500 mL
Finely grated gingerroot (or 1/4 tsp., 1 mL, ground ginger)	1 tsp.	5 mL
Garlic clove, crushed (or 1/4 tsp., 1 mL, powder)	1	1
Green onions, chopped	3	3
Bamboo shoots, cut into matchsticks	2/3 cup	150 mL
Soy sauce	1 tsp.	5 mL
Mandarin Pancakes, page 122		
Hoisin sauce	1 1/2 tbsp.	25 mL

Marinade: Combine first 6 ingredients in medium bowl. Stir until sugar is dissolved.

Add pork strips. Stir 2 or 3 times. Marinate at room temperature for 20 minutes.

Cover mushrooms with boiling water in small bowl. Let stand for 20 minutes until softened. Rinse. Drain. Squeeze dry. Discard stems. Cut caps into matchsticks. Set aside.

(continued on next page)

92 Main Courses

Fork-beat eggs, salt and pepper together in small bowl. Pour into greased frying pan. Scramble-fry until chunky but still moist. Turn out onto plate. Break up larger pieces.

Heat wok or frying pan until hot. Add cooking oil. Add pork strips, discarding marinade. Stir-fry for 3 minutes. Add mushrooms, suey choy, ginger, garlic, green onion, bamboo shoots and second amount of soy sauce. Stir-fry for 3 minutes. Add egg mixture. Cook until heated through. Makes 4 cups (1 L).

Lightly brush Mandarin Pancakes with hoisin sauce on 1 side. Place 1/4 cup (60 mL) pork mixture in center of each pancake. Fold up, envelope-style. Makes 16 rolls.

1 roll: 101 Calories; 3.1 g Total Fat; 287 mg Sodium; 8 g Protein; 10 g Carbohydrate; 1 g Dietary Fiber

Pictured on page 90.

Pork And Peppers (Japan)

Quite colorful with a delicate flavor. Very satisfying.

Cooking oil	1 tbsp.	15 mL
Pork loin (or pork tenderloin), thinly sliced (or cubed)	1 1/2 lbs.	680 g
Cubed green pepper (about 2 medium)	1 1/2 cups	375 mL
Cubed red pepper (about 2 medium)	1 1/2 cups	375 mL
Cubed yellow pepper (about 2 medium)	1 1/2 cups	375 mL
Green onions, cut into 3 inch (7.5 cm) pieces	6	6
Soy sauce	1/4 cup	60 mL
Sake (rice wine) or sherry (or alcohol-free sherry)	1/4 cup	60 mL
Granulated sugar	2 tbsp.	30 mL
Cornstarch	1 tbsp.	15 mL

Heat wok or frying pan until hot. Add cooking oil. Add pork slices. Stir-fry for about 2 minutes until browned.

Add next 4 ingredients. Stir-fry for about 6 minutes until peppers are tender-crisp.

Stir soy sauce, sake and sugar into cornstarch in small bowl until smooth. Stir into pork mixture until boiling and thickened. Serves 6.

1 serving: 241 Calories; 5.4 g Total Fat; 792 mg Sodium; 29 g Protein; 16 g Carbohydrate; 2 g Dietary Fiber

Pictured on page 90.

Braised Pork (China)

Soy-flavored sauce with tender pork. Good with either
Nutty Steamed Rice, page 129, or Orange-Flavored Rice, page 130.

Cooking oil	1 tbsp.	15 mL
Boneless pork loin (or pork tenderloin), cut into small cubes	1 lb.	454 g
Piece of gingerroot (1 inch, 2.5 cm), thinly sliced	1	1
Green onions, cut into 1 inch (2.5 cm) pieces	3	3
Soy sauce	1/4 cup	60 mL
Granulated sugar	1 1/2 tsp.	7 mL
Sherry (or alcohol-free sherry)	2 tsp.	10 mL
Pepper	1/4 tsp.	1 mL
Garlic powder	1/8 tsp.	0.5 mL
Boiling water	1 1/2 cups	375 mL
Thinly sliced carrot	1 cup	250 mL
Frozen cut green beans	1 cup	250 mL

Heat wok or frying pan until hot. Add cooking oil. Add pork cubes. Stir-fry for about 2 minutes until browned.

Add next 8 ingredients. Stir. Cover. Simmer for about 45 minutes until pork cubes are tender.

Add carrot. Cover. Simmer for 8 minutes.

Add green beans. Cover. Simmer for 4 minutes until vegetables are tender. Makes 2 2/3 cups (650 mL).

1/2 cup (125 mL): 163 Calories; 4.8 g Total Fat; 880 mg Sodium; 22 g Protein; 7 g Carbohydrate; 1 g Dietary Fiber

 To test spices and herbs for freshness, smell them. No aroma, no flavor.

Sweet And Sour Pork (China)

A colorful and popular dish that tastes so good.
Great with Stir-Fried Rice, page 127.

Boneless pork, cut bite size	2 lbs.	900 g
Water, to cover		
Salt	2 tsp.	10 mL
Medium carrots, cubed	2	2
Large onions, cubed	2	2
Medium green peppers, cubed	2	2
SWEET AND SOUR SAUCE		
Brown sugar, packed	1 1/2 cups	375 mL
All-purpose flour	1/4 cup	60 mL
White vinegar	1/2 cup	125 mL
Water	1/4 cup	60 mL
Soy sauce	2 tbsp.	30 mL
Ketchup	1 tbsp.	15 mL
Ground ginger	1/4 tsp.	1 mL
Garlic powder	1/4 tsp.	1 mL

Combine pork, water and salt in large saucepan. Bring to a boil. Reduce heat. Cover. Simmer for about 50 minutes until pork is almost tender.

Add carrot and onion. Bring to a boil. Cook for 30 minutes.

Add green pepper. Bring to a boil. Cook until green pepper is tender-crisp. Drain. Set aside.

Sweet And Sour Sauce: Mix brown sugar and flour well in medium saucepan. Stir in remaining 6 ingredients until smooth. Heat and stir on medium until boiling and thickened. Pour over pork mixture. Toss until well coated. Transfer to warmed platter or bowl. Serves 6.

1 serving: 584 Calories; 19.3 g Total Fat; 884 mg Sodium; 32 g Protein; 72 g Carbohydrate; 2 g Dietary Fiber

Lumpia (Philippines)

Pronounced LOOM-pee-ah. Bright green and orange accents in these lightly crisped rolls. The dark golden sauce really makes this dish. Make it a complete meal with Chicken Salad, page 106, and Cassava Biscuits, page 124.

Vermicelli nest	1	1
Boiling water	6 cups	1.5 L
Salt	2 tsp.	10 mL
BROWN SAUCE		
Water	3/4 cup	175 mL
Cornstarch	1 tbsp.	15 mL
Granulated sugar	1/4 cup	60 mL
Oyster sauce	3 tbsp.	50 mL
Garlic powder	1/4 tsp.	1 mL
Lemon juice	2 tbsp.	30 mL
Beef bouillon powder	1 tsp.	5 mL
Chopped onion	1/2 cup	125 mL
Garlic clove, minced (or 1/4 tsp., 1 mL, powder)	1	1
Cooking oil	1 tsp.	5 mL
Lean ground pork	1/2 lb.	225 g
Frozen cut green beans	1 cup	250 mL
Grated carrot	1 cup	250 mL
Pepper	1/8 tsp.	0.5 mL
Soy sauce	2 tbsp.	30 mL
Large egg	1	1
Egg roll wrappers	16	16
Cooking oil	2 tsp.	10 mL

Cook vermicelli, boiling water and salt in medium uncovered saucepan for 2 minutes. Drain. Cut vermicelli into 2 inch (5 cm) lengths. Set aside.

Brown Sauce: Combine first 7 ingredients in small saucepan. Heat and stir until boiling and thickened. Makes 1 cup (250 mL) sauce.

Sauté onion and garlic in cooking oil in frying pan until onion is soft.

Combine next 6 ingredients in medium bowl. Add to onion mixture. Scramble-fry until ground pork is no longer pink. Add vermicelli. Stir.

(continued on next page)

Place 1/3 cup (75 mL) each of pork mixture near 1 corner of each wrapper. Roll up, tucking in sides. Cook, 4 at a time, seam side down, in 1/4 of cooking oil in large frying pan for 1 to 1 1/2 minutes per side until golden. Serve with Brown Sauce. Serves 8.

1 serving: 343 Calories; 9.5 g Total Fat; 1209 mg Sodium; 13 g Protein; 54 g Carbohydrate; 1 g Dietary Fiber

Pork Fiddlehead Stir-Fry (Japan)

Fiddlehead ferns, sometimes called ostrich fern or pohole, grace this unusual, yet yummy, Japanese dish.

Cooking oil	1 tbsp.	15 mL
Pork tenderloin, cut julienne	1/2 lb.	225 g
Fresh (or frozen, thawed) fiddleheads (see Tip, below)	10 oz.	285 g
Peeled, julienned acorn squash	2 cups	500 mL
Shredded bok choy, lightly packed	3 cups	750 mL
SAUCE		
Ketchup	1/2 cup	125 mL
Worcestershire sauce	2 tbsp.	30 mL
Sesame (or cooking) oil	1 tsp.	5 mL
Ground ginger	1 tsp.	5 mL

Heat wok or frying pan until hot. Add cooking oil. Add pork. Stir-fry for 2 minutes.

Add fiddleheads and squash. Stir-fry for about 4 minutes until fiddleheads and squash are fairly tender.

Add bok choy. Stir-fry for about 1 minute until heated through.

Sauce: Stir all 4 ingredients in small cup. Add to pork mixture. Heat and stir until heated through. Makes 6 cups (1.5 L). Serves 4.

1 serving: 202 Calories; 6.6 g Total Fat; 535 mg Sodium; 18 g Protein; 21 g Carbohydrate; 4 g Dietary Fiber

To shop for fiddleheads, be sure they are tightly wound small, firm scrolls that are a bright green color. To store, place in a resealable plastic bag and keep in the refrigerator up to 3 days. Fiddleheads are more available from mid-April to mid-July.

Pad Thai (Thailand)

There are many versions of this common dish. The key ingredients are rice stick noodles, meat and vegetables flavored with fish sauce and/or shrimp. Sold by street vendors at any time day or night. You can use whichever you choose—chicken, shrimp, beef, pork, tofu—cut bite size as most Thai food is eaten with a fork and spoon.

Package of medium rice stick noodles (16 oz., 454 g)	1/2	1/2
Boiling water, to cover		
Cooking oil	2 tbsp.	30 mL
Garlic cloves, minced (or 3/4 tsp., 4 mL, powder)	3	3
Lean ground pork	4 oz.	113 g
Chopped raw shrimp, packed	1/2 cup	125 mL
Fish sauce	1 tbsp.	15 mL
Sambal oelek (chili paste)	1 tsp.	5 mL
Brown sugar, packed	2 tsp.	10 mL
Large eggs	2	2
Fish sauce	1 tbsp.	15 mL
Fresh lime, cut in half	1	1
Fresh bean sprouts	4 oz.	113 g
Green onions, sliced	4	4
Unsalted peanuts, coarsely chopped	1/4 cup	60 mL

Chopped fresh bean sprouts, for garnish
Chopped unsalted peanuts, for garnish
Chopped fresh cilantro, for garnish
Diced English cucumber, with peel, for garnish
Lemon wedges, for garnish
Lime wedges, for garnish

Cover noodles with boiling water. Let stand for 30 minutes until softened. Drain thoroughly. Set aside.

(continued on next page)

Heat wok or frying pan until very hot. Add cooking oil. Add garlic. Stir-fry until golden.

Add ground pork. Stir-fry until browned.

Add shrimp. Stir-fry until shrimp is pink.

Add first amount fish sauce, sambal oelek and brown sugar. Stir. Make a well in center.

Add eggs to well. Break yolks. Cook, without stirring, until partially set. Stir-fry until set. Push aside.

Add noodles. Stir-fry until heated through. Add second amount fish sauce. Stir. Squeeze juice from lime halves over mixture.

Add bean sprouts, green onion and peanuts. Stir-fry until heated through. Arrange on platter.

Top with bean sprouts, peanuts, cilantro, cucumber and lemon and lime wedges. Makes 6 cups (1.5 L).

1 cup (250 mL): 346 Calories; 14.2 g Total Fat; 414 mg Sodium; 15 g Protein; 40 g Carbohydrate; 2 g Dietary Fiber

---

Spicy Grilled Pork (Korea)

*Traditionally, this flavorful pork is well cooked, almost charred, on a grill.
Add Asparagus Sesame, page 137, to make this a meal.*

MARINADE

Sambal oelek (chili paste)	1 - 2 tbsp.	15 - 30 mL
Sesame (or cooking) oil	4 tsp.	20 mL
Liquid honey	2 tbsp.	30 mL
Garlic cloves, minced (or 3/4 tsp., 4 mL, powder)	3	3
Green onions, sliced	2	2
Boneless pork loin, cut across grain into 1/4 inch (6 mm) slices	1 lb.	454 g

Marinade: Combine first 5 ingredients in medium bowl.

Add pork strips. Stir. Cover. Marinate in refrigerator for at least 1 hour, stirring occasionally. Broil for about 2 minutes per side until well cooked. Serves 4.

1 serving: 303 Calories; 18.9 g Total Fat; 59 mg Sodium; 23 g Protein; 10 g Carbohydrate; trace Dietary Fiber

Lemon Grass Pork (Vietnam)

Contrasts subtle lemon grass, sharp chili and beautiful colors.
Good with Nuoc Cham, page 121.

Rice vermicelli	8 oz.	225 g
Boiling water, to cover		
Cooking oil	1 tbsp.	15 mL
Medium onion, halved lengthwise and thinly sliced crosswise	1	1
Garlic cloves, minced (or 1/2 tsp., 2 mL, powder)	2	2
Thinly sliced pork strips	1 lb.	454 g
Stalk of lemon grass	1	1
Fish sauce	1 1/2 tbsp.	25 mL
Granulated sugar	1 tsp.	5 mL
Chili sauce	2 tbsp.	30 mL
Cayenne pepper, dash (optional)		
Thinly sliced green onion	2 tbsp.	30 mL
Julienned carrot	1/4 cup	60 mL
Thinly slivered red pepper	1/4 cup	60 mL
Cilantro sprigs, for garnish		

Cover vermicelli with boiling water in small bowl. Let stand for 2 minutes. Drain. Set aside.

Heat wok or frying pan until hot. Add cooking oil. Add onion and garlic. Stir-fry for 2 minutes. Transfer to medium bowl.

Add 1/2 of pork strips to hot wok. Stir-fry for 2 to 3 minutes until no longer pink. Add to onion mixture. Stir-fry remaining pork strips until no longer pink. Leave in wok.

Remove outer leaves and rough tops of lemon grass, leaving about 3 to 4 inches (7.5 to 10 cm) root. Place on cutting surface. Press root with flat of knife. Chop finely. Add to pork strips in wok.

Add fish sauce, sugar, chili sauce and cayenne pepper. Stir. Add onion mixture and any juices. Stir-fry for about 2 minutes until pork strips are coated and sauce is slightly thickened. Makes 3 cups (750 mL). Place 1 cup (250 mL) vermicelli in each of 4 individual bowls. Divide pork mixture over vermicelli.

Arrange green onion, carrot and red pepper over pork mixture. Garnish with cilantro. Serves 4.

1 serving: 511 Calories; 18.4 g Total Fat; 503 mg Sodium; 28 g Protein; 57 g Carbohydrate; 2 g Dietary Fiber

Pictured on page 54.

Main Courses

Pork Chop Suey (China)

A pretty dish with a slightly sweet and peppery taste.
Serve with steamed rice or Stir-Fried Rice, page 127.

Lean boneless pork loin chops, cut into 1/8 inch (3 mm) strips	3/4 lb.	340 g
Cooking oil	1 tbsp.	15 mL
Water	1/2 cup	125 mL
Cornstarch	2 tsp.	10 mL
Beef bouillon powder	2 tsp.	10 mL
Brown sugar, packed	1 tbsp.	15 mL
Soy sauce	2 tsp.	10 mL
Salt	1 tsp.	5 mL
Pepper	1/8-1/4 tsp.	0.5-1 mL
Cooking oil	1 tsp.	5 mL
Diced celery	1/2 cup	125 mL
Medium onion, slivered (or chopped)	1	1
Medium carrots, grated	2	2
Small green pepper, slivered	1	1
Fresh bean sprouts	2 cups	500 mL

Sauté pork strips in first amount of cooking oil in wok or frying pan until browned and no longer pink. Transfer to medium bowl.

Stir water into cornstarch in small bowl until smooth. Add bouillon powder, brown sugar, soy sauce, salt and pepper. Stir. Set aside.

Add second amount of cooking oil to hot wok. Add celery, onion and carrot. Stir-fry for about 3 minutes until almost tender.

Add green pepper and bean sprouts. Stir-fry for 2 minutes. Add pork strips. Stir cornstarch mixture. Stir into pork mixture until boiling and thickened. Makes 4 1/2 cups (1.1 L).

3/4 cup (175 mL): 162 Calories; 6.6 g Total Fat; 764 mg Sodium; 14 g Protein; 12 g Carbohydrate; 2 g Dietary Fiber

Paré Pointer
Before beginning to paint the shed he put on all his jackets. The can clearly says to be sure to put on three coats.

Vegetarian Thai Noodles (Thailand)

Coconut milk combats the spicy red curry paste, while providing a delicious sauce for the noodles. This will work using a milder green chili paste as well.

Wide rice stick noodles	8 oz.	225 g
Boiling water, to cover		
Cooking oil	2 tbsp.	30 mL
Garlic cloves, minced (or 1/2 tsp., 2 mL, powder)	2	2
Thai red curry paste	1-1 1/2 tsp.	5-7 mL
Fish sauce	1 tbsp.	15 mL
Oyster sauce	1 tbsp.	15 mL
Low-sodium soy sauce	1 tbsp.	15 mL
Brown sugar, packed	1 tbsp.	15 mL
Rice vinegar	1 tbsp.	15 mL
Medium onion, thinly sliced lengthwise	1	1
Sliced celery	1/2 cup	125 mL
Medium carrot, cut julienne	1	1
Sliced mushrooms	2/3 cup	150 mL
Small broccoli florets	2 cups	500 mL
Fresh pea pods	24	24
Coconut milk	1 cup	250 mL
Cooking oil	2 tsp.	10 mL
Large eggs, fork-beaten	2	2
Chopped fresh sweet basil (or 3/4 tsp., 4 mL, dried)	1 tbsp.	15 mL
Salt, sprinkle		
Freshly ground pepper, sprinkle		
Fresh bean sprouts	1 cup	250 mL
Sliced green onion	2 tbsp.	30 mL
Chopped peanuts	2 tbsp.	30 mL

Cover noodles with boiling water in large bowl. Let stand for 30 minutes until softened. Drain well. Cut into shorter lengths. Set aside.

Heat wok or frying pan until hot. Add cooking oil. Add garlic. Stir-fry for about 30 seconds until golden.

Add curry paste. Stir-fry until fragrant.

Add fish sauce, oyster sauce, soy sauce, brown sugar and rice vinegar. Heat and stir until bubbling.

(continued on next page)

Add next 6 ingredients. Stir. Cook, uncovered, on high for 3 to 5 minutes, stirring occasionally, until vegetables are tender-crisp.

Add noodles and coconut milk. Heat and stir until heated through. Transfer to platter. Keep warm.

Add second amount of cooking oil in hot wok. Add egg. Swirl in wok to make thin layer. Sprinkle with basil, salt and pepper. Cook on medium until egg is firm. Remove to cutting board. Roll up, jelly roll-style. Cut crosswise into thin shreds. Arrange on top of noodle mixture.

Top with bean sprouts, green onion and peanuts. Makes 9 cups (2.25 L).

1 cup (250 mL): 258 Calories; 12.6 g Total Fat; 349 mg Sodium; 6 g Protein; 32 g Carbohydrate; 2 g Dietary Fiber

Egg Foo Yong (China)

Reminiscent of an omelet. Mild soy-flavored sauce, slightly sweet.

SAUCE

Water	2/3 cup	150 mL
Cornstarch	1 tbsp.	15 mL
Soy sauce	1 tbsp.	15 mL
Granulated sugar	1 tsp.	5 mL
Vegetable bouillon powder	1 tsp.	5 mL
Ketchup (optional)	1 tsp.	5 mL
Large eggs	8	8
Salt	1/2 tsp.	2 mL
Freshly ground pepper	1/8 tsp.	0.5 mL
Ground ginger	1/2 tsp.	2 mL
Fresh bean sprouts, cut in half	1 cup	250 mL
Finely chopped onion	1/2 cup	125 mL
Cooking oil	1 tbsp.	15 mL
Frozen peas	2/3 cup	150 mL

Sauce: Stir water into cornstarch in small saucepan until smooth. Add soy sauce, sugar, bouillon powder and ketchup. Heat and stir until boiling and thickened. Keep warm. Makes 3/4 cup (175 mL) sauce.

Beat eggs, salt, pepper and ginger together in medium bowl. Add bean sprouts. Stir.

Sauté onion in cooking oil in frying pan for about 2 minutes until soft.

Add peas. Sauté until heated through. Cool slightly. Stir into egg mixture. Spoon about 1/4 cup (60 mL) egg mixture into frying pan. Cook both sides until browned. Do not burn. Repeat with remaining egg mixture. Serve with 1 tbsp. (15 mL) sauce over each omelet. Makes 10 omelets.

1 omelet: 93 Calories; 5.5 g Total Fat; 345 mg Sodium; 6 g Protein; 5 g Carbohydrate; 1 g Dietary Fiber

Japanese Primavera (Japan)

Great texture in this spicy hot dish.
The eggs can be omitted for the dedicated vegetarian.

Rice vermicelli	9 oz.	255 g
Boiling water, to cover		
Water	1/2 cup	125 mL
Cornstarch	2 1/2 tsp.	12 mL
Oyster sauce	1/4 cup	60 mL
Soy sauce	1/4 cup	60 mL
Granulated sugar	4 tsp.	20 mL
Garlic powder	1/2 tsp.	2 mL
Cayenne pepper	1/2 tsp.	2 mL
Sesame (or cooking) oil	1 tbsp.	15 mL
Broccoli florets	2 cups	500 mL
Medium carrots, cut into matchsticks	2	2
Fresh pea pods	6 oz.	170 g
Sliced fresh mushrooms	2 cups	500 mL
Can of baby corn, drained and chopped	14 oz.	398 mL
Sesame seeds, toasted (see Tip, page 63)	2 tbsp.	30 mL

Cover vermicelli with boiling water in large bowl. Let stand for 10 minutes until softened. Drain. Set aside.

Stir second amount of water into cornstarch in small bowl until smooth. Add next 5 ingredients. Stir. Set aside.

Heat wok or frying pan until hot. Add sesame oil. Add broccoli and carrot. Stir-fry until tender-crisp.

Add remaining 4 ingredients. Stir-fry for 2 minutes. Stir cornstarch mixture. Stir into broccoli mixture until boiling and thickened. Serve over vermicelli. Makes 10 cups (2.5 L).

1 cup (250 mL): 191 Calories; 2.9 g Total Fat; 1035 mg Sodium; 5 g Protein; 38 g Carbohydrate; 3 g Dietary Fiber

Pictured on page 89.

Double Crunch Salad (Asia)

Such a pretty salad! Dressing is orange-flavored with an exotic hint of sesame.
Keep extra dressing in the refrigerator for up to ten days.

DRESSING

Garlic cloves (or 1/2 tsp., 2 mL, powder)	2	2
Green onion, chopped	1	1
Frozen concentrated orange juice, thawed	1/2 cup	125 mL
Cold water	1/4 cup	60 mL
Low-sodium soy sauce	2 tbsp.	30 mL
Dark corn syrup	1 tbsp.	15 mL
Sesame seeds, toasted (see Tip, page 63)	1 tbsp.	15 mL
Lime juice	1 tbsp.	15 mL
Finely grated gingerroot (or 1/2 tsp., 2 mL, ground ginger)	2 tsp.	10 mL
Sesame (or cooking) oil	1 tsp.	5 mL
Sambal oelek (chili paste)	1/2 tsp.	2 mL

SALAD

Thinly shredded red cabbage	3 cups	750 mL
Thinly sliced celery	2/3 cup	150 mL
Green onions, thinly sliced	2	2
Small yellow or orange pepper, seeded and cut into thin slivers	1	1
Fresh bean sprouts	1 cup	250 mL
Slivered almonds, toasted (see Tip, page 63)	1/4 cup	60 mL

Dressing: Process first 11 ingredients in food processor or blender until no large pieces of garlic or green onion remain. Let stand at room temperature for 30 minutes to blend flavors. Makes 1 1/4 cups (300 mL) dressing.

Salad: Toss cabbage, celery, green onion, yellow pepper and bean sprouts together in large bowl. Drizzle with 1/2 cup (125 mL) dressing. Toss to coat.

Sprinkle with almonds. Makes 6 cups (1.5 L). Serves 6.

1 serving: 122 Calories; 4.2 g Total Fat; 189 mg Sodium; 4 g Protein; 20 g Carbohydrate; 3 g Dietary Fiber

HOT CHICKEN CRUNCH: Grill or broil 2 boneless, skinless chicken breast halves (about 1/4 lb., 113 g, each), basting several times with 1/4 cup (60 mL) dressing, until no longer pink inside. Thinly slice chicken while still hot and lay several slices over individual servings of salad. Serves 4 as a luncheon salad.

Chicken Salad (Philippines)

Very tropical and refreshing. Good with Lumpia, page 96.

Unpeeled baby potatoes	8	8
Baby carrots	12	12
Water		
Salt	1/4 tsp.	1 mL
Boneless, skinless chicken breast halves (about 2), cooked and chopped (or can of flaked chicken, 6 1/2 oz., 184 g, drained)	1/2 lb.	225 g
Green onions, thinly sliced	2	2
Diced fresh (or canned) mango	1 cup	250 mL
Medium coconut (optional)	1 - 2 tbsp.	15 - 30 mL
Light mayonnaise	3 tbsp.	50 mL
White vinegar	1 tsp.	5 mL
Milk	1 tsp.	5 mL
Granulated sugar	1/4 tsp.	1 mL

Cook potatoes and carrots in water and salt in medium saucepan until tender. Drain. Cool enough to handle. Cut into quarters. Cool completely in large bowl.

Add chicken, green onion, mango and coconut. Toss lightly.

Mix remaining 4 ingredients in small cup. Add to chicken mixture. Stir to coat. Chill until ready to serve. Makes 3 2/3 cups (900 mL).

1/2 cup (125 mL): 100 Calories; 4.7 g Total Fat; 176 mg Sodium; 6 g Protein; 12 g Carbohydrate; 1 g Dietary Fiber

Pictured on page 107.

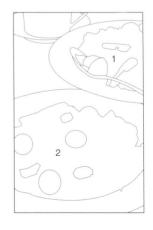

1. Chicken Salad, this page (Philippines)
2. Sweet And Sour Vegetables, page 138 (Malaysia)

Props Courtesy Of: Mikasa Home Store
The Bay

Daikon Carrot Salad (Japan)

A refreshing salad with a bit of crunch. Fine shreds make for a nice appearance.
Use a hand grater or grater blade on a food processor for shredding.
Try with Chicken Teriyaki, page 63.

Peeled and finely shredded daikon radish	3 1/3 cups	825 mL
Finely shredded carrot	1/3 cup	75 mL
Salt	1 1/2 tsp.	7 mL
Rice (or white) vinegar	1/4 cup	60 mL
Granulated sugar	3 tbsp.	50 mL
Sesame seeds, toasted (see Tip, page 63)	1 tsp.	5 mL

Toss radish, carrot and salt together in large bowl. Let stand for
10 minutes. Knead until soft. Squeeze dry.

Combine rice vinegar and sugar in small cup. Stir until sugar is dissolved.
Pour over radish mixture. Toss until well coated.

Sprinkle with sesame seeds. Makes 2 cups (500 mL).

1/2 cup (125 mL): 62 Calories; 0.5 g Total Fat; 910 mg Sodium; 1 g Protein; 15 g Carbohydrate;
2 g Dietary Fiber

Pictured on page 89.

1. Chicken Noodle Salad,
   page 110 (China)
2. Minty Pawpaw Salad,
   page 116 (Thailand)

Props Courtesy Of: Artifacts
                    Cherison Enterprises Inc.
                    Dansk Gifts

Salads

Chicken Noodle Salad (China)

An excellent combination of shapes and sizes with a
light vinaigrette dressing. Wonderful sesame oil finish.

Boneless, skinless chicken breast halves (about 2)	1/2 lb.	225 g
Water, to cover		
VINAIGRETTE DRESSING		
White vinegar	2 tbsp.	30 mL
Granulated sugar	3 tbsp.	50 mL
Sesame (or cooking) oil	1 tsp.	5 mL
Dry mustard	1/4 tsp.	1 mL
Soy sauce	1 tbsp.	15 mL
Onion powder	1/4 tsp.	1 mL
Cooking oil	1/2 tsp.	2 mL
Large egg, fork-beaten	1	1
Fresh bean sprouts	2 cups	500 mL
Thinly sliced romaine lettuce	2 cups	500 mL
Sesame seeds, toasted (see Tip, page 63)	2 tbsp.	30 mL
Chow mein noodles	1 cup	250 mL
Green onions, chopped	2	2
Chow mein noodles, for garnish	1/2 cup	125 mL

Cook chicken in water in large saucepan for about 18 minutes until no pink remains and juices run clear. Drain. Cool. Cut into strips. Chill until ready to assemble salad.

Vinaigrette Dressing: Combine first 6 ingredients in small bowl. Stir until sugar is dissolved. Makes 1/4 cup (60 mL) dressing.

Heat cooking oil in frying pan on medium. Add egg. Cover. Cook until set. Turn out onto cutting surface. Cool. Cut into thin strips. Cut strips into 2 inch (5 cm) lengths. Chill until ready to assemble salad.

Combine bean sprouts, lettuce and sesame seeds in large bowl. Add first amount of chow mein noodles and green onion. Toss to mix. Add chicken and dressing. Toss until well coated. Turn into serving bowl.

Top with egg strips and second amount of chow mein noodles. Makes 5 1/2 cups (1.4 L).

1 cup (250 mL): 182 Calories; 7.3 g Total Fat; 245 mg Sodium; 14 g Protein; 17 g Carbohydrate; 2 g Dietary Fiber

Pictured on page 108.

Gado-Gado (Indonesia)

GAH-doh GAH-doh is a full meal salad with a spicy dressing. Add bread as a go-with.

DRESSING

Fresh small red chili (seeds and ribs removed for less heat), chopped (see Tip, page 121)	1	1
Garlic clove, minced (or 1/4 tsp., 1 mL, powder)	1	1
Piece of gingerroot (1/8 × 1 inch, 0.3 × 2.5 cm), peeled	1	1
Salt	1/2 tsp.	2 mL
Pepper	1/8 tsp.	0.5 mL
Smooth peanut butter	1/2 cup	125 mL
Water	1/2 cup	125 mL
Granulated sugar	2 tsp.	10 mL
Cooking oil	2 tbsp.	30 mL
Cooking oil	1 tbsp.	15 mL
Firm tofu, cut into 3/4 inch (2 cm) cubes (about 1 cup, 250 mL)	1/2 lb.	225 g
Medium English cucumber, with peel, thinly sliced	1	1
Fresh bean sprouts	1 cup	250 mL
Shredded cabbage	1 cup	250 mL
Fresh green beans, cooked	1/2 lb.	225 g
Small red onion, thinly sliced	1	1
Medium tomato, diced	1	1
Hard-boiled eggs, quartered	3	3
Salted peanuts, toasted (see Tip, page 63)	1/4 cup	60 mL
Flake coconut	1/4 cup	60 mL

Dressing: Process first 9 ingredients in blender until smooth. Makes 1 1/4 cups (300 mL) dressing.

Heat wok or frying pan until hot. Add second amount of cooking oil. Add tofu. Stir-fry for about 4 minutes until golden brown. Remove to paper towel to drain. Set aside.

Combine cucumber, bean sprouts, cabbage, green beans, onion and tomato in large bowl. Drizzle with dressing. Toss.

Place egg and tofu on top. Sprinkle with peanuts and coconut. Serve immediately. Makes 11 cups (2.75 L).

1 cup (250 mL): 217 Calories; 16.7 g Total Fat; 221 mg Sodium; 10 g Protein; 10 g Carbohydrate; 3 g Dietary Fiber

Spicy Radish Salad (Asia)

Color and texture galore! Serve as an accompaniment to a not-so-spicy
main course, such as Chicken And Asparagus, page 67, or
Rolled Sole In Coconut Sauce, page 80, for a nice balance.

Daikon radish, peeled	8 oz.	225 g
Coarse (pickling) salt	2 tsp.	10 mL
Small carrot	1	1
Jicama, peeled	8 oz.	225 g
Green onions, cut julienne	2	2
Medium English cucumber, with peel, cut julienne	1/2	1/2

DRESSING

Sesame (or cooking) oil	4 tsp.	20 mL
Rice vinegar	1/4 cup	60 mL
White corn syrup	2 tbsp.	30 mL
Frozen concentrated orange juice, thawed	2 tbsp.	30 mL
Garlic cloves, crushed (or 1/2 tsp., 2 mL, powder)	2	2
Fresh small red chilies (seeds and ribs removed for less heat), finely chopped (see Tip, page 121)	2	2
Paprika	1 tsp.	5 mL
Mixed baby salad greens	4 cups	1 L
Package of enoki mushrooms	3 1/2 oz.	100 g

Cut radish into long fine strands with garnishing tool or vegetable peeler. Place in colander. Sprinkle with salt. Mix. Let stand for 15 minutes. Rinse with cold water. Squeeze dry. Place in medium bowl.

Cut carrot and jicama into long fine strands. Add to radish. Add green onion and cucumber.

Dressing: Combine first 7 ingredients in small bowl. Let stand for 30 minutes to blend flavors. Add to radish mixture. Toss to coat. Makes 5 cups (1.25 L).

Arrange greens on 8 chilled salad plates. Top with radish mixture and mushrooms. Makes 8 servings.

1 serving: 81 Calories; 2.6 g Total Fat; 620 mg Sodium; 2 g Protein; 14 g Carbohydrate; 2 g Dietary Fiber

Pictured on front cover.

Japanese Lettuce Salad (Japan)

Serve this salad on chilled plates to keep the lettuce extra crisp. Remember, the presentation is as important as the taste and the taste is very good. Keep extra dressing in the refrigerator for up to one week.

GINGER DRESSING

Rice vinegar	1/4 cup	60 mL
Water	1 tbsp.	15 mL
Low-sodium soy sauce	1 tbsp.	15 mL
Chili sauce	1 tbsp.	15 mL
Cooking oil	1 tbsp.	15 mL
Finely chopped gingerroot (or 3/4 tsp., 4 mL, ground ginger)	1 tbsp.	15 mL
Sesame (or cooking) oil	2 tsp.	10 mL
Brown sugar, packed	1 tsp.	5 mL
Green onion, cut into 8 pieces	1	1
Celery rib, chopped	1	1
Torn iceberg lettuce	3 cups	750 mL
Tomato slices, 1/4 inch (6 mm) thick (or 12 cherry tomato roses, see Tip, below)	6	6
English cucumber slices, with peel, diagonally cut 1/4 inch (6 mm) thick	6	6
Medium carrot, sliced (see Garnishes, page 11)	1	1

Ginger Dressing: Put first 10 ingredients into blender. Process on high until smooth. Makes 3/4 cup (175 mL) dressing.

Arrange remaining 4 ingredients, in order given, on 6 chilled salad plates. Drizzle 1 tbsp. (15 mL) dressing over each just before serving. Serves 6.

1 serving: 58 Calories; 4 g Total Fat; 98 mg Sodium; 1 g Protein; 5 g Carbohydrate; 1 g Dietary Fiber

 To make a tomato rose, peel a firm ripe tomato with a sharp knife, making a continuous 1/2 to 3/4 inch (1.2 to 2 cm) wide and 12 inch (30 cm) long strip of peel. Coil the skin in the palm of your hand and spread the "petals" to form a rose.

Great Thai Salad (Thailand)

North Americanized version of Som Tam, a green papaya salad, commonly sold by street vendors. Make sure the salad is arranged on a very large platter so all the vegetables and fruit can be seen. Thai food is always beautifully garnished with fresh ingredients.

THAI DRESSING		
Finely chopped onion	1 tbsp.	15 mL
Garlic clove, minced (or 1/4 tsp., 1 mL, powder)	1	1
Cooking oil	1 tsp.	5 mL
Shrimp paste	1 tsp.	5 mL
Flake coconut	2 tbsp.	30 mL
Unsalted peanuts, chopped	1/4 cup	60 mL
Finely grated gingerroot (or 1/4 tsp., 1 mL, ground ginger)	1 tsp.	5 mL
Brown sugar, packed	1/2 cup	125 mL
Fresh small red chili (seeds and ribs removed for less heat, see Tip, page 121)	1	1
Water	1 cup	250 mL
Freshly squeezed lime juice (about 1 small)	2 tbsp.	30 mL
Frozen french-cut green beans	3 cups	750 mL
Boiling water, to cover		
Shredded green cabbage	1 1/2 cups	375 mL
Shredded red cabbage	1 1/2 cups	375 mL
Can of sliced water chestnuts, drained	8 oz.	227 mL
Under-ripe medium papaya, thinly sliced and cut julienne	1	1
Star fruit, ridges removed and cut into 1/4 inch (6 mm) thick slices	1	1
Medium English cucumber, with peel, cut thinly on diagonal and then in half	1/2	1/2

Thai Dressing: Sauté onion and garlic in cooking oil in frying pan until onion is soft. Stir in shrimp paste. Cool. Turn into blender.

(continued on next page)

Add coconut, peanuts, ginger, brown sugar, chili and 2 tbsp. (30 mL) water. Process until consistency of fine paste. Add remaining water. Process until combined. Pour into small saucepan. Bring to a boil. Boil hard, uncovered, for about 10 minutes until mixture is slightly thickened. Cool.

Add lime juice. Stir. Makes 1 1/3 cups (325 mL) dressing.

Blanch green beans by plunging into boiling water in large saucepan for about 2 minutes until bright green and tender-crisp. Drain. Chill quickly under cold running water.

Arrange green cabbage around outside rim of very large serving platter. Place red cabbage in center. Arrange green beans over red cabbage. Place water chestnuts on top of green beans. Top with papaya. Arrange star fruit around papaya. Arrange cucumber around star fruit. Drizzle with 1/2 of dressing. Serve with remaining dressing on the side. Serves 8.

1 serving: 169 Calories; 4.4 g Total Fat; 18 mg Sodium; 4 g Protein; 32 g Carbohydrate; 4 g Dietary Fiber

Pictured on page 53 and back cover.

Potato Raita (India)

A RI-tah should cool the mouth from spicy foods.
This one cools and pleases at the same time. A unique potato salad.

Unpeeled medium potatoes	4	4
Water		
Finely chopped English cucumber, with peel	1 cup	250 mL
Plain yogurt	3/4 cup	175 mL
Lemon juice	1 tsp.	5 mL
Granulated sugar	1/2 tsp.	2 mL
Salt	1/2 tsp.	2 mL
Ginger paste (or finely grated gingerroot)	1/4 tsp.	1 mL
Chopped fresh mint leaves (optional)	1/4 cup	60 mL
Chopped fresh cilantro (optional)	1 tbsp.	15 mL

Cook potatoes in water in large saucepan until tender. Drain. Cool. Peel. Cut into 1/2 inch (12 mm) cubes. Transfer to large bowl.

Mix remaining 8 ingredients in small bowl. Add to potato. Stir well. Makes 5 cups (1.25 L).

3/4 cup (175 mL): 93 Calories; 0.6 g Total Fat; 203 mg Sodium; 3 g Protein; 19 g Carbohydrate; 1 g Dietary Fiber

Salads

Minty Pawpaw Salad (Thailand)

Papaya and papaw are both sometimes referred to as "pawpaw" even though they are very different. Papaya is readily available in North America; papaw is quite rare. Butter lettuce leaves make a perfect cup to hold this salad.

DRESSING

Lemon (or lime) juice	2 tbsp.	30 mL
Garlic clove, minced (or 1/4 tsp., 1 mL, powder)	1	1
Finely grated gingerroot (or 1/8 tsp., 0.5 mL, ground ginger)	1/2 tsp.	2 mL
Fish sauce	2 tbsp.	30 mL
Golden corn (or cane) syrup	1 tbsp.	15 mL
Chili sauce	1 tbsp.	15 mL
Dried crushed chilies	1/8 tsp.	0.5 mL
Ripe large papayas, peeled, seeded and diced	2	2
Small red onion, cut into paper-thin slices	1	1
Small red pepper, slivered	1	1
Fresh mint leaves, chopped	1/3 cup	75 mL
Butter lettuce leaves	12 - 20	12 - 20

Dressing: Combine first 7 ingredients in small dish. Let stand at room temperature for 30 minutes to blend flavors. Makes 1/3 cup (75 mL) dressing.

Place papaya, onion, red pepper, mint and dressing in large bowl. Toss gently until well coated. Makes 4 cups (1 L) salad.

Line small bowls with 3 to 5 lettuce leaves each. Add 1 cup (250 mL) salad to each. Serves 4.

1 serving: 104 Calories; 0.4 g Total Fat; 539 mg Sodium; 3 g Protein; 25 g Carbohydrate; 4 g Dietary Fiber

Pictured on page 108.

Paré Pointer

He knew that town backwards, so that explains why he drove in reverse.

Salads

Dipping Sauce (Korea)

Anything is good dipped in this sweet and sour sauce. Serve with Pajeon, page 15, Kujolp'an, page 20, or Battered Meatballs, page 32.

Sesame seeds, toasted (see Tip, page 63) and crushed	1 tsp.	5 mL
Low-sodium soy sauce	2/3 cup	150 mL
Apple cider vinegar	2 tbsp.	30 mL
Brown sugar, packed	2 tsp.	10 mL
Cayenne pepper, sprinkle		
Finely sliced green onion	1 tbsp.	15 mL

Combine all 6 ingredients in small bowl. Makes about 1 cup (250 mL).

1 tbsp. (15 mL): 9 Calories; 0.1 g Total Fat; 328 mg Sodium; 1 g Protein; 2 g Carbohydrate; trace Dietary Fiber

Pictured on page 17.

Miso Dipping Sauce (Japan)

Miso has a pleasant and slightly unusual taste. The darker the color, the more intense the flavor. Different but good. Serve with Deep-Fried Spring Rolls, page 28.

Miso (fermented soybean paste)	1 tbsp.	15 mL
Soy sauce	2 tbsp.	30 mL
Water	1 tbsp.	15 mL
Rice vinegar	2 tsp.	10 mL
Paprika	1 tsp.	5 mL
Brown sugar, packed	1 tsp.	5 mL
Cayenne pepper	1/4 tsp.	1 mL

Chopped fresh chives, for garnish

Mash miso with fork in small bowl. Gradually stir in soy sauce and water until well blended and smooth.

Add rice vinegar, paprika, brown sugar and cayenne pepper. Mix well. Let stand for 15 minutes to blend flavors.

Garnish with chives. Makes 1/4 cup (60 mL).

1 tbsp. (15 mL): 20 Calories; 0.3 g Total Fat; 649 mg Sodium; 1 g Protein; 3 g Carbohydrate; trace Dietary Fiber

Spring Roll Dipping Sauce (Vietnam)

A pretty dipping sauce with flecks of carrot and chilies. Lots of flavor. Serve with Deep-Fried Spring Rolls, page 28, or Vietnamese Spring Rolls, page 29.

Water	1 cup	250 mL
Rice vinegar	3 tbsp.	50 mL
Fish sauce	1/4 cup	60 mL
Finely grated carrot	1 tbsp.	15 mL
Granulated sugar	2 tsp.	10 mL
Garlic clove, crushed (or 1/4 tsp., 1 mL, powder)	1	1
Dried crushed chilies	1/4 tsp.	1 mL

Combine all 7 ingredients in small bowl. Let stand for 15 minutes to blend flavors. Makes 1 1/2 cups (375 mL).

1 tbsp. (15 mL): 4 Calories; 0 g Total Fat; 176 mg Sodium; trace Protein; 1 g Carbohydrate; trace Dietary Fiber

Pictured on page 125.

Two Ginger Sauce (Japan)

Japanese influence, using rice vinegar and lots of gingerroot. Excellent served over Japan-Style Rice, page 129, or as a sauce for meat.

Coarsely chopped gingerroot	1/3 cup	75 mL
Low-sodium soy sauce	1/4 cup	60 mL
Rice vinegar	2 tbsp.	30 mL
Dark corn syrup	2 tbsp.	30 mL
Sesame (or cooking) oil	2 tbsp.	30 mL
Lemon juice	1 tbsp.	15 mL
Dry mustard	1 tsp.	5 mL
Ground ginger	1 tsp.	5 mL
White grape juice	1/4 cup	60 mL

Put all 9 ingredients into blender. Process on high for several minutes until ginger is puréed. Store in jar with tight-fitting lid in refrigerator for up to 1 week. Stir well before serving. Makes about 1 cup (250 mL).

1 tbsp. (15 mL): 29 Calories; 1.7 g Total Fat; 128 mg Sodium; trace Protein; 3 g Carbohydrate; trace Dietary Fiber

Peanut Sauce (Thailand)

A perfect texture for dipping. Delicious with any skewered meat.
Good with Pleated Purses, page 31, Bulgogi, page 59, Meatballs In
Tasty Broth, page 62, or Thai Pizza In A Garlic Crust, page 66.

Chopped fresh cilantro stems	2 tbsp.	30 mL
Garlic cloves, crushed (or 1/2 tsp., 2 mL, powder)	2	2
Sambal oelek (chili paste)	1-1 1/2 tsp.	5-7 mL
Fish sauce	1 tsp.	5 mL
Sesame (or cooking) oil	1 tsp.	5 mL
Peanut butter	1/3 cup	75 mL
Golden corn (or cane) syrup	3 tbsp.	50 mL
Rice vinegar	2 tbsp.	30 mL
Coconut milk	1/2 cup	125 mL
Lime juice	2 tbsp.	30 mL
Unsalted peanuts, toasted (see Tip, page 63) and finely chopped, for garnish	1 tbsp.	15 mL

Grind first 4 ingredients together using mortar and pestle (see Tip, below) until paste-like consistency.

Heat sesame oil in small saucepan until hot. Add paste. Cook until just fragrant.

Add peanut butter, syrup, vinegar, coconut milk and lime juice. Heat and stir on medium until starting to bubble. Remove from heat. Cool to room temperature.

Sprinkle with peanuts. Makes 1 1/8 cups (280 mL).

1 tbsp. (15 mL): 54 Calories; 4.1 g Total Fat; 47 mg Sodium; 1 g Protein; 4 g Carbohydrate; trace Dietary Fiber

Pictured on page 144.

 tip   *To save the time and effort of grinding herbs with a mortar and pestle, use a coffee grinder. Purchase an inexpensive coffee grinder for the sole purpose of grinding herbs. Do not use your regular coffee grinder or the herb taste will linger in your coffee. To clean your coffee grinder, regularly grind a few pieces of fresh bread. Works like a charm!*

Lime Ginger Sauce (Thailand)

Amber-colored sauce with a candied ginger flavor.
Serve warm over cut-up fresh fruit, Surprise Crab Cakes, page 19,
Pleated Purses, page 31, or Sweet Fried Bananas, page 50.

Brown sugar, packed	2/3 cup	150 mL
Water	3 tbsp.	50 mL
Hard margarine (or butter)	1 tbsp.	15 mL
Freshly squeezed lime juice (about 1 small)	2 tbsp.	30 mL
Finely grated gingerroot (or 1/4 tsp., 1 mL, ground ginger)	1 tsp.	5 mL

Combine brown sugar, water and margarine in small heavy saucepan. Heat and stir on medium until boiling and sugar is dissolved. Boil, without stirring, for about 2 minutes until slightly reduced.

Stir in lime juice and ginger. Keep sauce warm until ready to serve. Makes 1/2 cup (125 mL).

1 tbsp. (15 mL): 84 Calories; 1.4 g Total Fat; 24 mg Sodium; trace Protein; 19 g Carbohydrate; trace Dietary Fiber

Nuoc Leo (Vietnam)

Pronounced noo-AHK lee-OH, this Vietnamese Peanut Sauce is different from
Thai peanut sauces in that the base is tomato and coconut milk is omitted.
As well, you'll find this sauce not as sweet as the Thai version.
Good with Vietnamese Spring Rolls, page 29.

Garlic cloves, minced (or 1/2 tsp., 2 mL, powder)	2	2
Cooking (or chili-flavored) oil	2 tsp.	10 mL
Sambal oelek (chili paste)	1/2 tsp.	2 mL
Crunchy peanut butter	1/3 cup	75 mL
Can of tomato sauce	7 1/2 oz.	213 mL
Brown sugar, packed	2 tsp.	10 mL
Fish sauce	1 tbsp.	15 mL

(continued on next page)

Sauté garlic in cooking oil in small saucepan until soft and golden.

Add sambal oelek and peanut butter. Stir. Add tomato sauce, brown sugar and fish sauce. Stir. Cover. Simmer for 5 minutes until slightly reduced and thickened. Cool. Makes about 7/8 cup (200 mL).

1 tbsp. (15 mL): 51 Calories; 3.8 g Total Fat; 194 mg Sodium; 2 g Protein; 3 g Carbohydrate; 1 g Dietary Fiber

---

Nuoc Cham (Vietnam)

Pronounced noo-AHK CHAHM, the heat of this Chili Dipping Sauce is determined by the kind and quantity of chilies used. It's best to make this ahead of time and let stand before determining if the taste suits your preference. Good with Pajeon, page 15, Meatballs In Tasty Broth, page 62, or Lemon Grass Pork, page 100.

Garlic cloves (or 1/2 tsp., 2 mL, powder)	2	2
Fresh small red chilies (seeds and ribs removed for less heat, see Tip, below)	1 - 6	1 - 6
Brown sugar, packed	1 tbsp.	15 mL
Fish sauce	1/4 cup	60 mL
Rice vinegar	3 tbsp.	50 mL
Lime (or lemon) juice	2 tbsp.	30 mL
Water	2 tbsp.	30 mL

Put all 7 ingredients into blender. Process until garlic and chilies are finely chopped but not puréed. Let stand for at least 10 minutes to blend flavors. Chill for 1 to 2 days. Makes 2/3 cup (150 mL).

1 tbsp. (15 mL): 13 Calories; 0 g Total Fat; 395 mg Sodium; 1 g Protein; 3 g Carbohydrate; trace Dietary Fiber

Pictured on page 18.

 tip *To wash chilies, rinse in cold water. Do not use hot water as this causes irritating fumes to rise toward your eyes and nose. As well, wear gloves when chopping chilies and avoid touching your eyes.*

Mandarin Pancakes (China)

A thin, crêpe-like pancake that is perfect for Moo Shu Pork, page 92.

All-purpose flour	2 1/3 cups	575 mL
Boiling water	1 cup	250 mL
Sesame (or cooking) oil	4 tsp.	20 mL

Combine flour and boiling water in medium bowl. Mix until soft ball is formed. Add more flour if dough is too sticky to handle. Turn out onto lightly floured surface. Knead for 5 to 8 minutes until smooth and elastic. Cover with plastic wrap. Let stand for 20 minutes. Divide dough into 16 equal portions. Shape each portion into a ball. Flatten into 4 inch (10 cm) circles.

Brush top of 1 circle with sesame oil. Place another circle on top. Roll into 6 inch (15 cm) circle on lightly floured surface (see Tip, below). Repeat with remaining circles. Keep covered with plastic wrap to prevent drying out. Heat non-stick frying pan until hot. Cook double pancakes, 1 at a time, for about 30 seconds until a few brown spots appear. Turn over. Cook for 30 seconds. Do not over cook or they will become brittle. Separate into 2 pancakes while still hot. Fold each in half and set on greased plate or tray. Cover. To serve, steam for about 5 minutes or cover individual pancakes with damp paper towel and microwave on high (100%) for 10 to 20 seconds until warm and soft. Makes 16 pancakes.

1 pancake: 78 Calories; 1.3 g Total Fat; trace Sodium; 2 g Protein; 14 g Carbohydrate; 1 g Dietary Fiber

Pictured on page 90.

 tip *When rolling out Mandarin pancakes, rotate and turn over frequently to maintain an even thickness and roundness. The pancakes can be prepared in advance and stored in a resealable plastic bag in the refrigerator for up to 2 days.*

Roti (India)

Traditionally, ROH-tee is one of the food staples that East Indian girls learn to make at a young age. Spread with jam or sprinkle with cinnamon sugar for a sweet treat.

Fine whole wheat (roti) flour (or regular whole wheat flour)	2 cups	500 mL
Ghee	1 tbsp.	15 mL
Salt	1/2 tsp.	2 mL
Warm water, approximately	2/3 cup	150 mL
Ghee	1 tbsp.	15 mL

Rub flour, first amount of ghee and salt together with fingers in medium bowl or directly on work surface until ghee is incorporated into flour.

Slowly add warm water, while mixing with your fingers, until dough clings together. Knead on lightly floured surface until smooth. Cover with damp cloth or plastic wrap. Let stand for 15 minutes. Divide dough into 15 equal portions. Lightly roll on floured surface. Flatten into small circles. Keep covered to prevent drying out. Roll out each circle on floured surface to 5 to 6 inch (12.5 to 15 cm) roti. Stack 4 or 5 roti, rolled side up. Cook, 1 at a time, in hot non-stick frying pan, rolled side down, on high for 20 seconds until puffy spots appear over surface. Flip over onto wire rack placed over element on high. Cook on wire rack over direct heat for 10 seconds. Roti should puff up in several places as it cooks. Flip over again to stack on plate.

Lightly brush top with some ghee. Repeat with remaining dough and ghee. Makes 15 roti.

1 roti: /1 Calories; 1.9 g Total Fat; 98 mg Sodium; 2 g Protein; 12 g Carbohydrate; 2 g Dietary Fiber

Pictured on page 36.

Cassava Biscuits (Philippines)

These light and fluffy biscuits are best eaten fresh or if frozen, reheated slightly. Try with Chicken And Pork Stew, page 79, or Lumpia, page 96.

All-purpose flour	1 cup	250 mL
Cassava (tapioca) flour	1 cup	250 mL
Granulated sugar	1 1/2 tbsp.	25 mL
Baking powder	4 tsp.	20 mL
Salt	1/8 tsp.	0.5 mL
Hard margarine (or butter)	1/2 cup	125 mL
Milk	3/4 cup	175 mL

Measure first 5 ingredients into large bowl. Cut in margarine until mixture is crumbly.

Add milk. Mix until soft ball is formed. Turn out onto lightly floured surface. Knead 8 times. Roll out to 3/4 inch (2 cm) thickness. Cut into 2 inch (5 cm) circles. Arrange in single layer on ungreased baking sheet. Bake in 450°F (230°C) oven for about 12 minutes until risen and golden. Makes about 16 biscuits.

1 biscuit: 133 Calories; 6.4 g Total Fat; 189 mg Sodium; 2 g Protein; 17 g Carbohydrate; 1 g Dietary Fiber

1. Seafood Dim Sum, page 91 (China)
2. Deep-Fried Spring Rolls, page 28 (Vietnam)
3. Surprise Crab Cakes, page 19 (Vietnam)
4. Oi Kimchee, page 39 (Korea)
5. Spring Roll Dipping Sauce, page 118 (Vietnam)
6. Noodle Fan, page 11

Props Courtesy Of: Island Pottery
Chemainus Inc.

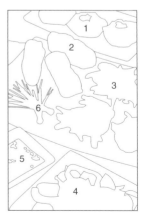

Side Dishes

Stir-Fried Rice (China)

The rice can be made ahead of time for quick preparation.
Really good with Ginger Beef, page 58, Sweet And Sour Pork, page 95,
or Pork Chop Suey, page 101.

Long grain white rice	1 cup	250 mL
Water	2 cups	500 mL
Large eggs	2	2
Salt	1/2 tsp.	2 mL
Pepper, just a pinch		
Cooking oil	2 tbsp.	30 mL
Green onions, chopped, for garnish	3	3

Rinse rice under cold water until water runs clear. Cook rice in water in covered medium saucepan until boiling. Reduce heat. Simmer for about 20 minutes, without lifting lid, until water is absorbed and rice is tender. Turn into large bowl. Cool.

Beat eggs, salt and pepper in medium bowl. Add to rice. Mix well.

Heat wok or frying pan until hot. Add cooking oil. Add rice mixture. Stir-fry until rice mixture is broken up and dried. Turn into serving bowl.

Sprinkle with green onion. Makes 3 1/4 cups (800 mL).

3/4 cup (175 mL): 256 Calories; 9 g Total Fat; 306 mg Sodium; 6 g Protein; 36 g Carbohydrate; trace Dietary Fiber

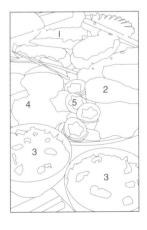

1. Spinach Chicken Teriyaki, page 75 (Japan)
2. Punjab Chicken, page 68 (India)
3. Saffron Vegetable Pulao, page 135 (India)
4. Honey Ginger Chicken, page 77 (Vietnam)
5. Carrot Stars, page 11

Props Courtesy Of: Fumiya Japanese
Food Store
Stokes

East Indian Coconut Rice (India)

*Fragrant basmati rice is made even more so with the addition of
cinnamon and cardamom. Serve as a bed for Sauced Halibut, page 82.*

Large onion, finely chopped	1	1
Celery rib, diced	1	1
Ghee	3 tbsp.	50 mL
Ground cinnamon	1/4 tsp.	1 mL
Ground cardamom	1/4 tsp.	1 mL
Turmeric	1/4 tsp.	1 mL
Salt	1 1/2 tsp.	7 mL
Basmati rice	2 cups	500 mL
Cans of light coconut milk (14 oz., 400 mL each)	2	2
Water	1/4 cup	60 mL

Sauté onion and celery in ghee in large saucepan until very soft.

Add cinnamon, cardamom, turmeric and salt. Stir.

Rinse rice under cold water until water runs clear. Drain well. Add to onion
mixture. Heat and stir on medium for about 2 minutes until rice is well
coated and turning golden.

Add coconut milk and water. Heat and stir until boiling. Reduce heat to
medium-low. Cover. Simmer for about 20 minutes, without lifting lid, until
liquid is absorbed and rice is tender. Makes 8 cups (2 L).

*3/4 cup (175 mL): 241 Calories; 10.2 g Total Fat; 388 mg Sodium; 4 g Protein; 33 g Carbohydrate;
1 g Dietary Fiber*

Pictured on page 71.

*For best results when cooking rice, choose a saucepan with a
tight-fitting lid to prevent steam escaping. Avoid lifting the lid or
stirring the rice while cooking. Better yet, put an automatic rice
cooker on your wish list. It cooks rice perfectly every time.*

Japan-Style Rice (Japan)

A very different method of cooking rice compared to the usual in North America. Turns out well even without the thirty minute soaking time. Serve with Teriyaki Meatballs, page 57, Spinach Chicken Teriyaki, page 75, Somen And Fish, page 83, or Two Ginger Sauce, page 118.

| Short grain white rice | 2 cups | 500 mL |
| Water | 2 1/4 cups | 550 mL |

Rinse rice under cold water until water runs clear. Combine rice and water in large saucepan. Cover. Let stand for 30 minutes. Bring to a boil on high. Reduce heat to low. Simmer for about 20 minutes, without lifting lid, until water is absorbed and rice is tender. Remove from heat. Keep covered. Let stand for 10 minutes. Makes 7 cups (1.75 L).

3/4 cup (175 mL): 163 Calories; 0.2 g Total Fat; trace Sodium; 3 g Protein; 36 g Carbohydrate; 0 g Dietary Fiber

Nutty Steamed Rice (China)

Nice nutty aroma and taste to this variation of steamed rice. Serve with Peppered Chicken, page 73, or Braised Pork, page 94.

Long grain white rice	1 cup	250 mL
Water	2 cups	500 mL
Chicken bouillon powder	2 tsp.	10 mL
Parsley flakes	2 tsp.	10 mL
Sliced almonds, toasted (see Tip, page 63)	1/4 cup	60 mL

Rinse rice under cold water until water runs clear. Place rice in medium saucepan. Add water, chicken bouillon and parsley flakes. Stir. Bring to a boil. Reduce heat to low. Cover. Simmer for about 20 minutes, without lifting lid, until water is absorbed and rice is tender.

Add almonds. Stir to combine. Makes 3 cups (750 mL).

3/4 cup (175 mL): 221 Calories; 3.8 g Total Fat; 330 mg Sodium; 5 g Protein; 41 g Carbohydrate; 1 g Dietary Fiber

Orange-Flavored Rice (China)

Very simple and very orangy.
Good with Peppered Chicken, page 73, or Braised Pork, page 94.

Long grain white rice	1 cup	250 mL
Prepared orange juice	1 cup	250 mL
Water	1 cup	250 mL
Chicken bouillon powder	1 tsp.	5 mL
Chopped chives	1 - 2 tsp.	5 - 10 mL
Pepper (white is best)	1/8 tsp.	0.5 mL

Rinse rice under cold water until water runs clear. Place rice in medium saucepan. Add orange juice, water and chicken bouillon. Stir. Bring to a boil. Reduce heat to medium-low. Cover. Simmer for about 30 minutes, without lifting lid, until liquid is absorbed and rice is tender.

Add chives and pepper. Stir. Makes 2 1/2 cups (625 mL).

3/4 cup (175 mL): 254 Calories; 0.6 g Total Fat; 200 mg Sodium; 5 g Protein; 56 g Carbohydrate;
1 g Dietary Fiber

Rice And Clams (Korea)

Subtly complements Tender Korean Beef, page 52,
and flavorful Bulgogi, page 59.

Short grain white rice	2 cups	500 mL
Can of baby clams, drained and liquid reserved	5 oz.	142 g
Rice vinegar	2 tsp.	10 mL
Sherry (or alcohol-free sherry)	2 tsp.	10 mL
Soy sauce	2 tsp.	10 mL
Water, approximately	1 1/3 cups	325 mL
Fresh bean sprouts, chopped	1 cup	250 mL
Green onion, sliced	1	1

Rinse rice under cold water until water runs clear. Place rice in medium saucepan.

(continued on next page)

Combine reserved clam liquid, rice vinegar, sherry and soy sauce in 4 cup (1 L) liquid measure. Add water to equal 3 cups (750 mL). Add to rice.

Add bean sprouts. Bring to a boil. Reduce heat to low. Cover. Simmer for about 20 minutes, without lifting lid, until liquid is absorbed and rice is tender.

Add clams and green onion. Stir. Cook, uncovered, for 5 minutes, stirring occasionally, until heated through. Makes 7 cups (1.75 L).

1 cup (250 mL): 252 Calories; 0.7 g Total Fat; 149 mg Sodium; 10 g Protein; 50 g Carbohydrate; trace Dietary Fiber

Pictured on page 144.

Thai Coconut Rice (Thailand)

Many Thai people prefer long grain white rice, but "sticky" or glutinous short grain rice is mainly eaten in Northern Thailand. Up to 1 cup (250 mL) each is eaten at most meals.

Can of coconut milk	14 oz.	400 mL
Can of condensed chicken broth	10 oz.	284 mL
Water	3/4 cup	175 mL
Salt	1/2 tsp.	2 mL
Long grain white rice	1 2/3 cups	400 mL
Grated lime peel	1/2 tsp.	2 mL
Sliced green onion	1/3 cup	75 mL
Flake coconut, toasted (see Tip, page 63), for garnish	2 tbsp.	30 mL

Rinse rice under cold water until water runs clear. Place coconut milk, broth, water and salt in medium saucepan. Stir. Bring to a boil. Add rice. Stir. Reduce heat. Cover. Simmer for 20 minutes, without lifting lid. Remove from heat. Let stand for 10 minutes until liquid is absorbed and rice is tender.

Sprinkle with lime peel and green onion. Stir gently with fork to distribute.

Sprinkle with coconut. Makes 5 cups (1.25 L).

3/4 cup (175 mL): 307 Calories; 13 g Total Fat; 473 mg Sodium; 7 g Protein; 42 g Carbohydrate; 1 g Dietary Fiber

Pictured on page 53 and back cover.

Green Bean Stir-Fry (Indonesia)

Nice contrast of colors and shapes and a nice blending of vegetables with coconut, garlic and ginger. Serve with Coco-Milk Chicken, page 70, or Cooked Whole Trout, page 81.

Cooking oil	2 tbsp.	30 mL
Garlic cloves, thinly sliced (or 1/2 tsp., 2 mL, powder)	2	2
Shallots, coarsely chopped	2	2
Fresh small red chili (seeds and ribs removed for less heat), thinly sliced (see Tip, page 121)	1	1
Bay leaves	2	2
Piece of gingerroot (1/4 inch, 6 mm), peeled	1	1
Salt	1/2 tsp.	2 mL
Green beans, cut into 2 inch (5 cm) pieces	1 lb.	454 g
Medium carrots, thinly sliced	2	2
Coconut milk	1/2 cup	125 mL

Heat wok or frying pan until hot. Add cooking oil. Add garlic, shallots, chilies, bay leaves, gingerroot and salt. Stir-fry for 2 minutes.

Add green beans and carrot. Stir-fry for 1 minute. Add coconut milk. Reduce heat to medium. Cook for about 6 minutes until vegetables are tender-crisp. Remove and discard bay leaves and gingerroot. Makes 4 cups (1 L).

1/2 cup (125 mL): 92 Calories; 6.8 g Total Fat; 162 mg Sodium; 2 g Protein; 8 g Carbohydrate; 2 g Dietary Fiber

Pictured on page 71.

String Beans (Japan)

Changes beans from ordinary to extraordinary in such an easy fashion. Complements Chicken Teriyaki, page 63, or Sake Fish, page 88.

Fresh (or frozen) whole green beans (about 5 cups, 1.25 L)	1 lb.	454 g
Boiling water		

(continued on next page)

Miso (fermented soybean paste)	1 tbsp.	15 mL
Brown sugar, packed	1 tbsp.	15 mL
Soy sauce	1 tsp.	5 mL
Sesame paste	2 tsp.	10 mL

Cook green beans in boiling water in large saucepan until tender-crisp. Drain.

Combine miso, brown sugar, soy sauce and sesame paste in small cup. Add to green beans. Toss until well coated. Makes 3 cups (750 mL). Serves 4.

1 serving: 74 Calories; 1.8 g Total Fat; 254 mg Sodium; 3 g Protein; 14 g Carbohydrate; 3 g Dietary Fiber

Dhal Curry (India)

Dhal is the Hindi word for lentils, of which there are many different kinds used in Indian cooking. Serve over rice for an easy vegetarian meal.

DHAL

Red lentils	1 cup	250 mL
Chopped onion	1 cup	250 mL
Turmeric	1/4 tsp.	1 mL
Garlic cloves, minced (or 1/2 tsp., 2 mL, powder)	2	2
Medium tomato, diced	1	1
White vinegar	2 tsp.	10 mL
Curry powder	4 tsp.	20 mL
Water	2 cups	500 mL
Salt	3/4 tsp.	4 mL

CRISP FRIED BROWN ONIONS

Ghee	1 tbsp.	15 mL
Chopped onion	1 cup	250 mL

Dhal: Combine first 8 ingredients in large saucepan, Bring to a boil. Cover. Cook on low for about 15 minutes, stirring frequently to prevent burning, until lentils are very soft but still hold their shape.

Add salt. Stir. Makes 3 1/2 cups (875 mL) Dhal.

Crisp Fried Brown Onions: Heat ghee in small frying pan until hot. Add onion. Sauté for about 15 minutes until crisp and browned. Sprinkle over Dhal before serving.

1/2 cup (125 mL): 140 Calories; 2.2 g Total Fat; 280 mg Sodium; 9 g Protein; 23 g Carbohydrate; 4 g Dietary Fiber

Nasi Goreng (Indonesia)

Nahg-SEE goh-REHNG is the Indonesian version of Chinese fried rice.
This is a meal in itself! Serve smaller portions with Coco-Milk Chicken, page 70,
or Cooked Whole Trout, page 81.

Diced onion	2/3 cup	150 mL
Diced celery	2/3 cup	150 mL
Cooking oil	1 tbsp.	15 mL
Diced cooked ham (about 2 1/2 oz., 71 g)	2/3 cup	150 mL
Cooked salad shrimp (about 2 1/4 oz., 64 g)	1/2 cup	125 mL
Cooking oil	1 tbsp.	15 mL
Large eggs, fork-beaten	2	2
Salt, sprinkle		
Freshly ground pepper, sprinkle		
Cooking oil	1 tbsp.	15 mL
Sweet soy sauce	1 tbsp.	15 mL
Ketchup	2 tsp.	10 mL
Cayenne pepper	1/4 tsp.	1 mL
Cold cooked long grain white rice	3 cups	750 mL
Crisp Fried Brown Onions, page 133 (optional)	3 tbsp.	50 mL

Sauté onion and celery in first amount of cooking oil in non-stick wok or frying pan for about 5 minutes until onion is soft.

Add ham and shrimp. Sauté for about 1 minute until heated through.

Push ham mixture aside, clearing a space in center of pan. Add second amount of cooking oil. Pour egg into center of pan. Sprinkle with salt and pepper. Cook for about 2 minutes, without stirring, until egg is firm enough to turn over. Turn egg over. Cook for just a few seconds. Dice egg with straight edge of pancake lifter. Combine with ham mixture.

Combine next 4 ingredients in small dish. Add to egg mixture. Stir.

Add 1/2 of rice. Use wet hands to break up rice as it's added to pan. Stir. Heat and toss on medium-high for 3 to 4 minutes until hot. Add remaining rice. Heat and toss for 10 minutes until rice is separated and heated through.

Garnish with Crisp Fried Brown Onions. Makes 4 cups (1 L).

3/4 cup (175 mL): 315 Calories; 11.8 g Total Fat; 528 mg Sodium; 13 g Protein; 38 g Carbohydrate; 1 g Dietary Fiber

Saffron Vegetable Pulao (India)

Pronounced poo-LAWOH, this could turn out to be one of your favorite ways to eat rice—colorful, textured and scrumptious. Turmeric is often substituted for very expensive saffron threads, but the flavor of the real thing is unmatched.

Finely chopped onion	1 1/2 cups	375 mL
Garlic clove, minced (or 1/4 tsp., 1 mL, powder)	1	1
Ghee	3 tbsp.	50 mL
Coarsely grated carrot	1/4 cup	60 mL
Fresh green beans, cut into 1 inch (2.5 cm) pieces	3/4 cup	175 mL
Diced red pepper	1/3 cup	75 mL
Basmati (or long grain white) rice, rinsed	2 cups	500 mL
Ground cumin	1/4 tsp.	1 mL
Ground cardamom	1/4 tsp.	1 mL
Ground ginger	1/4 tsp.	1 mL
Freshly ground pepper, heavy sprinkle		
Ground cloves, sprinkle		
Bay leaf	1	1
Boiling water	3 2/3 cups	900 mL
Saffron threads (or turmeric)	1/4 tsp.	1 mL
Salt	1/2 tsp.	2 mL
Chopped cashews, toasted (see Tip, page 63)	2 tbsp.	30 mL

Sauté onion and garlic in ghee in large heavy saucepan until onion is very soft and golden.

Stir in carrot, green beans and red pepper. Sauté for 3 minutes.

Add next 7 ingredients. Heat and stir until rice starts to brown.

Add boiling water and saffron threads. Stir. Cover. Simmer for 25 to 30 minutes until water is absorbed. Remove and discard bay leaf.

Add salt. Fluff with fork. Sprinkle with cashews. Makes 8 cups (2 L).

3/4 cup (175 mL): 188 Calories; 4.4 g Total Fat; 154 mg Sodium; 3 g Protein; 33 g Carbohydrate; 1 g Dietary Fiber

Pictured on page 126.

Cabbage Fry (Japan)

One of the best side dishes going! Slight crunchiness.
A must-try with Chicken Yakitori, page 78.

SAUCE		
Water	1/3 cup	75 mL
Cornstarch	2 tsp.	10 mL
Soy sauce	2 tbsp.	30 mL
Chicken bouillon powder	1 tsp.	5 mL
Salt	1/8 tsp.	0.5 mL
Pepper	1/4 tsp.	1 mL
Miso (fermented soybean paste)	1 tsp.	5 mL
Cooking oil	1 tbsp.	15 mL
Thinly sliced celery	1 1/2 cups	375 mL
Shredded cabbage	4 cups	1 L
Fresh bean sprouts	1 cup	250 mL
Green onions, sliced, for garnish	3	3
Sesame seeds, toasted (see Tip, page 63), for garnish	1 tbsp.	15 mL

Sauce: Stir water into cornstarch in small cup until smooth. Add soy sauce, bouillon powder, salt, pepper and miso. Mix well.

Heat wok or frying pan until hot. Add cooking oil. Add celery, cabbage and bean sprouts. Stir-fry for about 4 minutes until tender-crisp. Stir sauce. Add to cabbage mixture. Stir until boiling and thickened.

Garnish with green onion and sesame seeds. Makes 2 1/3 cups (575 mL).

3/4 cup (175 mL): 109 Calories; 5.8 g Total Fat; 984 mg Sodium; 4 g Protein; 12 g Carbohydrate; 3 g Dietary Fiber

Spiffy Carrots (Japan)

The simple addition of a few ingredients gives these carrots a sweet and nutty flavor. Try with Chicken Yakitori, page 78, or Sake Fish, page 88.

Medium carrots (about 1 lb., 454 g), sliced	7	7
Boiling water		

(continued on next page)

Miso (fermented soybean paste)	1 tbsp.	15 mL
Mayonnaise	1 tbsp.	15 mL
Granulated sugar	1 tbsp.	15 mL
Soy sauce	1 tsp.	5 mL
Sesame paste	1 tsp.	5 mL

Cook carrot in boiling water in medium saucepan until tender-crisp. Drain.

Combine miso and mayonnaise in small cup. Add sugar, soy sauce and sesame paste. Stir. Add to carrot. Toss until well coated. Makes 2 1/2 cups (625 mL).

1/2 cup (125 mL): 93 Calories; 3.2 g Total Fat; 251 mg Sodium; 2 g Protein; 15 g Carbohydrate; 3 g Dietary Fiber

---

Asparagus Sesame (Korea)

An excellent vegetable stir-fry that is complemented by the sesame flavor.
Serve warm or cold with Spicy Grilled Pork, page 99.

Sesame (or cooking) oil	1 tbsp.	15 mL
Sesame seeds	1 tbsp.	15 mL
Fresh asparagus, trimmed of tough ends and cut on diagonal into 1 1/2 inch (3.8 cm) pieces	1 lb.	454 g
Water	1/4 cup	60 mL
Soy sauce	1 tbsp.	15 mL
Chicken bouillon powder	1/2 tsp.	2 mL
Hot pepper sauce, dash		

Heat wok or frying pan until hot. Add sesame oil. Add sesame seeds and asparagus. Stir-fry for 1 to 2 minutes until asparagus is bright green.

Add water, soy sauce, bouillon powder and hot pepper sauce. Stir. Cover. Cook on medium for about 5 minutes until asparagus is tender-crisp. Remove asparagus with slotted spoon to bowl or plate. Boil liquid until reduced by half. Add asparagus. Toss. Makes 2 cups (500 mL).

1/2 cup (125 mL): 74 Calories; 4.9 g Total Fat; 346 mg Sodium; 3 g Protein; 6 g Carbohydrate; 2 g Dietary Fiber

Sweet And Sour Vegetables (Malaysia)

Very attractive dish, especially with sesame seeds. Quite a nip from the chili and
ginger. Similar to a pickle flavor. Try with Chicken Fried Noodles, page 68.

White vinegar	1/2 cup	125 mL
Apple cider vinegar	1/4 cup	60 mL
Water	1/3 cup	75 mL
Granulated sugar	1/3 cup	75 mL
Finely chopped lemon grass	1 tbsp.	15 mL
Finely chopped gingerroot (or 1/2 tsp., 2 mL, ground ginger)	1 1/2 tsp.	7 mL
Garlic cloves, minced (or 3/4 tsp., 4 mL, powder)	3	3
Turmeric	1/2 tsp.	2 mL
Sambal oelek (chili paste)	1 tsp.	5 mL
Medium carrots, thinly sliced	2	2
Medium English cucumber, with peel, thinly sliced	1/2	1/2
Cherry tomatoes, halved	12	12
Medium red onion, thinly sliced	1/2	1/2
Fresh bean sprouts	1 cup	250 mL
Sesame seeds, toasted (see Tip, page 63), optional	1 tsp.	5 mL

Combine first 4 ingredients in large saucepan. Bring to a boil. Reduce heat.

Add lemon grass, ginger, garlic, turmeric and sambal oelek. Stir. Simmer, uncovered, for 5 minutes. Cool.

Combine carrot, cucumber, tomato, onion and bean sprouts in medium bowl. Pour vinegar mixture over vegetables. Marinate in refrigerator for 8 to 24 hours. Drain. Discard marinade.

Sprinkle with sesame seeds. Makes 4 cups (1 L).

1/2 cup (125 mL): 65 Calories; 0.4 g Total Fat; 11 mg Sodium; 1 g Protein; 16 g Carbohydrate;
1 g Dietary Fiber

Pictured on page 107.

Stir-Fry Mixed Vegetables (Vietnam)

These vegetables combine so well. What a dish! Serve with Ga-Xao-Xa-Ot, page 65, Honey Ginger Chicken, page 77, or Tea-Poached Halibut, page 84.

Cooking oil	2 tbsp.	30 mL
Sesame (or cooking) oil	1 1/2 tsp.	7 mL
Garlic cloves, minced (or 1/2 tsp., 2 mL, powder)	2	2
Cauliflower florets	2 cups	500 mL
Medium leek (white and tender parts only), chopped	1	1
Bag of fresh spinach, chopped	10 oz.	285 g
Can of Chinese straw mushrooms, drained	14 oz.	398 mL
Soy sauce	1 tbsp.	15 mL
Sesame seeds, toasted (see Tip, page 63), for garnish	1 tbsp.	15 mL

Heat cooking oil and sesame oil in wok or frying pan until hot. Add garlic. Stir-fry for 10 seconds. Add cauliflower and leek. Stir-fry for 2 minutes. Add spinach and mushrooms. Cook for 2 minutes until spinach is wilted.

Add soy sauce. Stir well to combine.

Sprinkle with sesame seeds. Makes 4 cups (1 L).

1/2 cup (125 mL): 77 Calories; 5.2 g Total Fat; 275 mg Sodium; 3 g Protein; 7 g Carbohydrate; 3 g Dietary Fiber

 To help keep vegetables fresh in the refrigerator, trim away any damaged parts and place in resealable plastic bags.

Banh Pho Bo (Vietnam)

Ban-foh-BOH is a very common meal served in all homes. Street vendors in larger cities have this Beef Noodle Soup available all day. Very good.

Diced onion	1 cup	250 mL
Cooking oil	1 tbsp.	15 mL
Finely grated gingerroot (or 1/2 tsp., 2 mL, ground ginger)	2 tsp.	10 mL
Garlic clove, minced (or 1/4 tsp., 1 mL, powder)	1	1
Freshly ground pepper, sprinkle		
Ground cinnamon, sprinkle		
Cans of condensed chicken broth (10 oz., 284 mL, each)	2	2
Water	3 cups	750 mL
Beef bouillon powder	2 tsp.	10 mL
Grated carrot	1/2 cup	125 mL
Fresh small red chili (seeds and ribs removed for less heat), finely diced (see Tip, page 121)	1	1
Fish sauce	3 tbsp.	50 mL
Lime juice	1 tbsp.	15 mL
Beef tenderloin, very thinly sliced across the grain	5 oz.	140 g
Green onions, cut into 1 1/2 inch (3.8 cm) pieces and then cut julienne	2	2
Fresh bean sprouts	3 oz.	85 g
Small rice stick noodles	8 oz.	225 g
Boiling water, to cover		
Shredded fresh sweet basil (or cilantro), for garnish		

Sauté onion in cooking oil in large saucepan for 3 minutes until soft.

Add ginger, garlic, pepper and cinnamon. Stir. Sauté for 3 minutes until onion is browned.

Add next 5 ingredients. Stir. Reduce heat. Cover. Simmer for 10 minutes.

Add fish sauce, lime juice, beef, green onion and bean sprouts. Stir. Bring to a simmer. Simmer until beef is cooked. Turn off heat. Cover to keep hot. Makes 7 cups (1.75 L) soup.

(continued on next page)

140

Soups

Cover noodles with boiling water in large bowl. Let stand for 3 minutes until softened. Drain. Divide noodles among 6 large individual soup bowls. Ladle soup over top.

Garnish with basil. Serves 6.

1 serving: 270 Calories; 5.6 g Total Fat; 1371 mg Sodium; 14 g Protein; 41 g Carbohydrate; 2 g Dietary Fiber

Pictured on page 72.

Malaysian Beef Noodle Soup (Malaysia)

Rich brown broth with tender beef strips, translucent noodles, crunchy sprouts and contrasting egg wedges. And it tastes good too!

Medium onion, coarsely chopped	1	1
Garlic cloves, minced (or 3/4 tsp., 4 mL, powder)	3	3
Finely chopped gingerroot (or 1/4 tsp., 1 mL, ground ginger)	1 tsp.	5 mL
Cooking oil	1 tbsp.	15 mL
Cashews, finely chopped	1 tbsp.	15 mL
Ground coriander	1 tsp.	5 mL
Sambal oelek (chili paste)	1 tsp.	5 mL
Top sirloin steak, thinly sliced	1 lb.	454 g
Beef bouillon powder	2 tbsp.	30 mL
Water	6 cups	1.5 L
Pepper	1/2 tsp.	2 mL
Cooked rice noodles (about 4 1/2 oz., 125 g, dry)	2 cups	500 mL
Fresh bean sprouts	2 cups	500 mL
Hard-boiled eggs, cut into eighths	2	2
Green onions, chopped, for garnish	2	2

Sauté onion, garlic and ginger in cooking oil in wok or Dutch oven until onion is soft.

Add next 7 ingredients. Stir. Bring to a boil. Reduce heat. Simmer, uncovered, for 30 minutes. Makes 5 cups (1.25 L) soup.

Divide noodles and bean sprouts among 6 individual soup bowls. Ladle soup over top.

Top each with 3 egg wedges. Sprinkle with green onion. Serves 6.

1 serving: 301 Calories; 12.2 g Total Fat; 662 mg Sodium; 21 g Protein; 27 g Carbohydrate; 1 g Dietary Fiber

Sweet Corn Chicken Soup (China)

Flecks of green chives, corn kernels and ham throughout with nice chunks of chicken. Often served as the last course.

Water	3 cups	750 mL
Can of cream-style corn	14 oz.	398 mL
Slice of deli ham, diced	1	1
Boneless, skinless chicken breast halves (about 2), cooked and chopped	1/2 lb.	225 g
Soy sauce	1/2 tsp.	2 mL
Chicken bouillon powder	1 tbsp.	15 mL
Chopped fresh chives	2 tsp.	10 mL
Salt	1/8 tsp.	0.5 mL
Pepper	1/8 tsp.	0.5 mL
Water	2 tbsp.	30 mL
Cornstarch	1 tbsp.	15 mL
Sherry (or alcohol-free sherry), optional	1 tbsp.	15 mL
Large egg, fork-beaten	1	1

Combine first 9 ingredients in large saucepan. Heat and stir until boiling.

Stir second amount of water into cornstarch in small cup until smooth. Stir into chicken mixture until boiling and thickened.

Add sherry. Stir. Add egg in a very fine stream, stirring constantly. Makes 5 1/4 cups (1.3 L).

1 cup (250 mL): 145 Calories; 3 g Total Fat; 798 mg Sodium; 14 g Protein; 17 g Carbohydrate; 1 g Dietary Fiber

1. Tom Yam Goong (Hot And Sour Prawn Soup With Lemon Grass), page 146 (Thailand)
2. Meatballs In Tasty Broth, page 62 (Vietnam)

Props Courtesy Of: Artifacts
Winners Stores

142

Pork And Green Soup (China)

Just one spoonful of this vibrant green and white soup gives you a wonderful taste sensation. Very easy to prepare.

Lean ground pork	6 oz.	170 g
Chopped celery	1/2 cup	125 mL
Water	5 cups	1.25 L
Chicken bouillon powder	2 tbsp.	30 mL
Coarsely chopped bok choy (use mostly green part), lightly packed	3 1/2 cups	875 mL
Green onions, thinly sliced	2	2
Salt	1/8 tsp.	0.5 mL
Pepper	1/8 tsp.	0.5 mL

Combine ground pork, celery, water and bouillon powder in large saucepan. Heat and stir, breaking up pork, until boiling. Reduce heat. Cover. Simmer for 15 minutes.

Add bok choy and green onion. Stir. Simmer for 3 minutes. Add salt and pepper. Stir. Makes 7 cups (1.75 L).

1 cup (250 mL): 79 Calories; 5.7 g Total Fat; 647 mg Sodium; 5 g Protein; 2 g Carbohydrate; 1 g Dietary Fiber

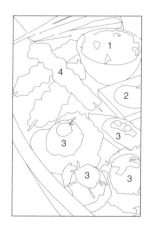

1. Rice And Clams, page 130 (Korea)
2. Peanut Sauce, page 119 (Thailand)
3. Sushi Lettuce Boats, page 25 (Japan)
4. Bulgogi (Korean Barbecued Beef), page 59 (Korea)

Props Courtesy Of: Artifacts
                   Osaka Japanese Restaurant
                   The Bay

Tom Yam Goong (Thailand)

Hot And Sour Prawn Soup With Lemon Grass is Thailand's favorite soup.
This is interesting and unusual. You may want to add more
Thai hot chili peppers for even more heat.

Stalks of lemon grass	2	2
Cans of condensed chicken broth (10 oz., 284 mL, each)	2	2
Water	3 cups	750 mL
Thai hot chili peppers (or 1/4 tsp., 1 mL, cayenne pepper)	2	2
Kaffir lime leaves, torn in half (or 1 tsp., 5 mL, grated lime peel)	3	3
Medium gingerroot, peeled and cut into 3/4 inch (2 cm) chunks	1	1
Freshly squeezed lime juice (about 1 medium)	1/4 cup	60 mL
Fish sauce	2 tbsp.	30 mL
Rice vinegar	1 tbsp.	15 mL
Can of Chinese straw mushrooms, drained	14 oz.	398 mL
Green onion, cut into 2 inch (5 cm) pieces and then cut julienne	1	1
Large prawns, peeled and deveined (see Tip, page 86)	1 lb.	454 g
Fresh cilantro, for garnish		

Remover dry straw-like pieces from lemon grass. Coarsely chop bottom 6 inches (15 cm).

Combine broth, water and lemon grass in large saucepan.

Bruise chili peppers by pounding with flat side of knife on hard surface. Add to lemon grass mixture. Add kaffir lime leaves and ginger. Stir. Bring to a boil. Reduce heat. Cover. Simmer for 15 minutes. Strain into medium bowl. Discard solids. Return broth to saucepan.

Add lime juice, fish sauce, rice vinegar and mushrooms to broth. Bring to a simmer.

(continued on next page)

Add green onion and prawns. Heat, uncovered, for 3 to 4 minutes until prawns are pink. Do not overcook.

Sprinkle cilantro over individual servings. Makes 6 cups (1.5 L).

1 cup (250 mL): 148 Calories; 2.7 g Total Fat; 1233 mg Sodium; 22 g Protein; 10 g Carbohydrate; 2 g Dietary Fiber

Pictured on page 143.

Osumashi (Japan)

AW-soo-MAH-shee is a clear soup with a light seaweed flavor.
Garnishes can be as sparse or as plentiful as you like.

Water	5 cups	1.25 L
Konbu (seaweed) pieces (2 inch, 5 cm, length)	4	4
Soy sauce	2 tbsp.	30 mL
Salt	1 tsp.	5 mL
Tofu cubes (1/2 inch, 12 mm, size)	25	25
Sprigs of parsley, for garnish	5	5
Chopped green onion, for garnish	5 tsp.	25 mL

Combine water and konbu in large saucepan. Heat until almost boiling. Do not boil. Remove from heat. Remove konbu with slotted spoon and discard.

Add soy sauce and salt to broth. Stir. Ladle into 5 individual soup bowls.

Divide tofu among bowls. Top each with parsley and 1 tsp. (5 mL) of green onion. Serves 5.

1 serving: 6 Calories; 0 g Total Fat; 898 mg Sodium; 1 g Protein; 1 g Carbohydrate; trace Dietary Fiber

QUICK OSUMASHI: Mix 1 envelope of single-serving osumashi with 1 cup (250 mL) boiling water.

Paré Pointer

There's a big difference between a coyote and a flea.
One howls on the prairie and one prowls on the hairy.

Chicken Shrimp Soup (Japan)

The broth has a pleasant mild soy sauce flavor and the chicken balls have a strong ginger flavor. A lovely combination.

Ground chicken	1/4 lb.	113 g
Soda cracker crumbs	2 tbsp.	30 mL
Water	1 tbsp.	15 mL
Soy sauce	1 tsp.	5 mL
Finely grated gingerroot (or 1/4 tsp., 1 mL, ground ginger), optional	1 tsp.	5 mL
Boiling water, to cover		
Boiling water	6 cups	1.5 L
Fish (or chicken) bouillon powder	2 tbsp.	30 mL
Fresh pea pods	18	18
Soy sauce	1 tbsp.	15 mL
Salt	1/8 tsp.	0.5 mL
Cooked large shrimp	12	12

Combine first 5 ingredients in small bowl. Shape slightly rounded tablespoonfuls into 12 balls. Place in single layer in bottom of large saucepan.

Cover chicken balls with first amount of boiling water. Bring to a boil. Boil for about 4 minutes until chicken is no longer pink. Drain. Transfer to separate small bowl.

Pour second amount of boiling water into same saucepan. Add bouillon powder, pea pods, soy sauce and salt. Bring to a boil. Boil for about 1 minute until pea pods are tender-crisp.

Add chicken balls and shrimp. Bring to a boil. Cook until heated through. Divide chicken balls, shrimp and pea pods among 6 individual soup bowls. Ladle broth over top. Serves 6.

1 serving: 68 Calories; 3.2 g Total Fat; 977 mg Sodium; 7 g Protein; 2 g Carbohydrate; trace Dietary Fiber

 To prevent freezer burn on poultry and other meats, always use freezer bags or containers. Freezer burn happens when moisture is lost, affecting the flavor and texture of the food.

Squash In Coconut Broth (Thailand)

Blending and cooking the garlic, green onion and sambal oelek intensifies the bold flavor of this soup. A rich soup as is, but the fat can be reduced by using light coconut milk. Serve in individual soup bowls with the meal or enjoy spooned over rice on a plate.

Garlic cloves, minced (or 1/2 tsp., 2 mL, powder)	2	2
Green onions, chopped	2	2
Sambal oelek (chili paste)	1/2 tsp.	2 mL
Shrimp paste	1 tsp.	5 mL
Sesame (or cooking) oil	2 tsp.	10 mL
Can of condensed chicken broth	10 oz.	284 mL
Water	2 cups	500 mL
Fish sauce	2 tsp.	10 mL
Chopped lemon grass	1 tbsp.	15 mL
Diced squash	3 cups	750 mL
Small cooked salad shrimp	1 1/2 cups	375 mL
Can of coconut milk	14 oz.	400 mL
Chopped fresh sweet basil (or 3/4 tsp., 4 mL, dried)	1 tbsp.	15 mL

Put first 5 ingredients into food processor. Process until smooth. Cook paste in large saucepan for about 1 minute until fragrant and slightly reduced.

Gradually stir broth and water into paste.

Add fish sauce, lemon grass and squash. Stir. Bring to a boil. Reduce heat. Cover. Simmer for about 10 minutes until squash is tender.

Stir in shrimp and coconut milk. Simmer for about 1 minute until just heated through.

Add basil. Stir. Makes 6 1/2 cups (1.6 L).

1 cup (250 mL): 195 Calories; 15 g Total Fat; 488 mg Sodium; 12 g Protein; 5 g Carbohydrate; 1 g Dietary Fiber

 For snowy white rice, add 1 tsp. (5 mL) vinegar to the water for every 1 cup (250 mL) rice.

Measurement Tables

Throughout this book measurements are given in Conventional and Metric measure. To compensate for differences between the two measurements due to rounding, a full metric measure is not always used. The cup used is the standard 8 fluid ounce. Temperature is given in degrees Fahrenheit and Celsius. Baking pan measurements are in inches and centimetres as well as quarts and litres. An exact metric conversion is given below as well as the working equivalent (Metric Standard Measure).

Spoons

Conventional Measure	Metric Exact Conversion Millilitre (mL)	Metric Standard Measure Millilitre (mL)
$1/8$ teaspoon (tsp.)	0.6 mL	0.5 mL
$1/4$ teaspoon (tsp.)	1.2 mL	1 mL
$1/2$ teaspoon (tsp.)	2.4 mL	2 mL
1 teaspoon (tsp.)	4.7 mL	5 mL
2 teaspoons (tsp.)	9.4 mL	10 mL
1 tablespoon (tbsp.)	14.2 mL	15 mL

Cups

Conventional Measure	Metric Exact Conversion Millilitre (mL)	Metric Standard Measure Millilitre (mL)
$1/4$ cup (4 tbsp.)	56.8 mL	60 mL
$1/3$ cup ($5^1/3$ tbsp.)	75.6 mL	75 mL
$1/2$ cup (8 tbsp.)	113.7 mL	125 mL
$2/3$ cup ($10^2/3$ tbsp.)	151.2 mL	150 mL
$3/4$ cup (12 tbsp.)	170.5 mL	175 mL
1 cup (16 tbsp.)	227.3 mL	250 mL
$4^1/2$ cups	1022.9 mL	1000 mL (1 L)

Dry Measurements

Conventional Measure Ounces (oz.)	Metric Exact Conversion Grams (g)	Metric Standard Measure Grams (g)
1 oz.	28.3 g	28 g
2 oz.	56.7 g	57 g
3 oz.	85.0 g	85 g
4 oz.	113.4 g	125 g
5 oz.	141.7 g	140 g
6 oz.	170.1 g	170 g
7 oz.	198.4 g	200 g
8 oz.	226.8 g	250 g
16 oz.	453.6 g	500 g
32 oz.	907.2 g	1000 g (1 kg)

Oven Temperatures

Fahrenheit (°F)	Celsius (°C)
175°	80°
200°	95°
225°	110°
250°	120°
275°	140°
300°	150°
325°	160°
350°	175°
375°	190°
400°	205°
425°	220°
450°	230°
475°	240°
500°	260°

Pans

Conventional Inches	Metric Centimetres
8x8 inch	20x20 cm
9x9 inch	22x22 cm
9x13 inch	22x33 cm
10x15 inch	25x38 cm
11x17 inch	28x43 cm
8x2 inch round	20x5 cm
9x2 inch round	22x5 cm
10x4$1/2$ inch tube	25x11 cm
8x4x3 inch loaf	20x10x7.5 cm
9x5x3 inch loaf	22x12.5x7.5 cm

Casseroles

CANADA & BRITAIN Standard Size Casserole	Exact Metric Measure	UNITED STATES Standard Size Casserole	Exact Metric Measure
1 qt. (5 cups)	1.13 L	1 qt. (4 cups)	900 mL
$1^1/2$ qts. ($7^1/2$ cups)	1.69 L	$1^1/2$ qts. (6 cups)	1.35 L
2 qts. (10 cups)	2.25 L	2 qts. (8 cups)	1.8 L
$2^1/2$ qts. ($12^1/2$ cups)	2.81 L	$2^1/2$ qts. (10 cups)	2.25 L
3 qts. (15 cups)	3.38 L	3 qts. (12 cups)	2.7 L
4 qts. (20 cups)	4.5 L	4 qts. (16 cups)	3.6 L
5 qts. (25 cups)	5.63 L	5 qts. (20 cups)	4.5 L

Photo Index

B

Banh Pho Bo. 72
Beef Noodle Soup 72
Bibimbap 54
Bulgogi. 144

C

Cabbage Kimchee. 17
Chicken Fried Noodles. 90
Chicken Noodle Salad 108
Chicken Salad 107
Chicken Yakitori. . . . . Front Cover
Chili Dipping Sauce. 18
Coconut Curry Shrimp . . . . 53, Back Cover
Coriander Chutney 36

D

Daikon Carrot Salad 89
Deep-Fried Spring Rolls 125
Dipping Sauce 17

E

East Indian Coconut Rice 71
East Indian Ice Cream 35

G

Gajar Halwa 35
Great Thai Salad . . . . 53, Back Cover
Green Bean Stir-Fry 71
Green Onion Pancakes 18

H

Honey Ginger Chicken. 126
Hot And Sour Prawn Soup
    With Lemon Grass 143

J

Japanese Primavera 89

K

Korean Barbecued Beef 144
Kujolp'an 17
Kulfi 35
Kung-Pao Chicken. 72

L

Lemon Grass Pork 54

M

Mandarin Pancakes 90
Meatballs In Tasty Broth. 143

Meatballs With Chutney Sauce. 18
Minty Pawpaw Salad 108
Moo Shu Pork. 90
Moo Shu Pork with Mandarin Pancakes . 90

N

Nuoc Cham 18

O

Oi Kimchee. 125

P

Pajeon 18
Peanut Sauce 144
Peppered Chicken 71
Pork And Peppers 90
Punjab Chicken. 126

R

Rice And Clams. 144
Rosy Ginger Pickle . . . . Front Cover
Roti 36

W

Saffron Vegetable Pulao 126
Sake Fish. 89
Seafood Dim Sum 125
Shrimp Mango Curry. 36
Spicy Radish Salad . . . . Front Cover
Spinach Chicken Teriyaki 126
Spring Roll Dipping Sauce 125
Strawberry Lassi 35
Strawberry Snow. 35
Surprise Crab Cakes. 125
Sushi Lettuce Boats 144
Sushi Stacks. . . . . Front Cover
Sweet And Sour Vegetables 107

T

Thai Coconut Rice. . . . . 53, Back Cover
Thai Dressing 53
Thai Pizza On A Garlic Crust 18
Tom Yam Goong. 143

V

Veggie Beef Rice Bowl 54

W

Whirl-A-Gig Sushi . . . . Front Cover

Tip Index

B

Bananas – to purchase 44
Bread – to clean coffee grinder 119
Bruising cardamom .41

C

Cardamom – to bruise 41
Chilies
– to avoid irritating fumes 121
– to clean 121
– to handle 121
Coconut – to toast .63
Coffee grinder
– to clean 119
– to grind herbs 119

D

Deveining shrimp 86

F

Fiddleheads
– availability 97
– to purchase 97
– to store 97
Fish
– to freshen frozen flavor 84
– to remove odors 83
– to shop for fresh 82
– to store 85
– to thaw 84
Freezer burn – to prevent 148
Fresh vegetables – to store 139

G

Grinding herbs 119

H

Herbs – to grind 119
Herbs – to determine freshness 94

K

Kimchee – for best results 33

M

Mandarin pancakes
– to make ahead 122
– to roll out 122
Mango – to purchase 48
Meat – to prevent freezer burn 148
Milk – to freshen frozen fish 84

N

Nuts – to toast 63

O

Odor – to remove .83

P

Poultry – to prevent freezer burn 148

R

Rice
– to achieve best results 128
– to make snowy white 149
Rose – to make from a tomato 113

S

Sesame seeds – to toast 63
Shrimp – to devein .86
Shrimp – to thaw 87
Spices – to determine freshness 94
Storing
– fish 85
– vegetables 139
Sushi – to get full benefit of flavor 25

T

Thawing – shrimp 87
Toasting – nuts, coconut, sesame seeds 63
Tomato rose – to make 113

V

Vegetables – to store 139
Vinegar – to make snowy white rice 149

W

Water – temperature to wash chilies 121

Recipe Index

A

Appetizers
Battered Meatballs. 32
Chicken Tikka 30
Deep-Fried Spring Rolls 28
Green Onion Pancakes. 15
Japanese Omelet 14
Kujolp'an. 20
Pajeon 15
Pakora 16
Pancake Batter. 20
Parsley Sushi Rice. 22
Pink Sushi Rice. 22
Pleated Purses 31
Rainbow Sushi. 27
Surprise Crab Cakes. 19
Sushi Lettuce Boats 25
Sushi Rice 22
Sushi Stacks. 23
Vegetable Samosas 26
Vietnamese Spring Rolls. 29
Whirl-A-Gig Sushi. 24
Yellow Sushi Rice 22
Asian Eggplant Stir-Fry 55
Asparagus, Chicken And 67
Asparagus Sesame. 137

B

Banana Pudding, Sweet 44
Bananas, Caramel 46
Bananas, Sweet Fried. 50
Banh Pho Bo. 140
Barbecued Beef, Korean 59
Batter, Pancake 20
Battered Meatballs 32
Beans, String. 132
Beef
Asian Eggplant Stir-Fry. 55
Banh Pho Bo 140
Beefy Spinach Noodles 60
Bibimbap. 51
Bulgogi. 59
Chap Jae 56
Ginger. 58
Korean Barbecued 59
Kujolp'an. 20
Malaysian Beef Noodle Soup 141
Meatballs In Tasty Broth. 62
Stir-Fry Beef And Noodles 56
Sukiyaki 61
Tender Korean 52
Teriyaki Meatballs 57
Veggie Beef Rice Bowl 51
Beef Noodle Soup. 140
Beef Teriyaki 63
Beef Yakitori 78
Beefy Spinach Noodles 60
Bibimbap 51
Biscuits, Cassava 124
Braised Pork 94
Breads
Cassava Biscuits 124
Green Onion Pancakes. 15

Mandarin Pancakes 122
Pajeon 15
Roti 123
Brown Sauce. 96
Bulgogi 59

C

Cabbage Fry 136
Cabbage Kimchee. 33
Cabbage With Fish, Coconut. 85
Caramel Bananas 46
Carrot Salad, Daikon 109
Carrots, Spiffy 136
Cassava Biscuits. 124
Chai, Indian 40
Chap Jae. 56
Chicken
Coco-Milk 70
Ga-Xao-Xa-Ot 65
Honey Ginger 77
Hot Chicken Crunch 105
Kung-Pao 76
Meatballs With Chutney Sauce . . . 64
Peppered. 73
Punjab. 68
Spicy Chicken With Lemon Grass. . 65
Spinach Chicken Teriyaki 75
Sweet Corn Chicken Soup 142
Thai Pizza On A Garlic Crust 66
Chicken And Asparagus. 67
Chicken And Pork Stew. 79
Chicken Curry Wraps. 74
Chicken Fried Noodles 68
Chicken Noodle Salad. 110
Chicken Salad 106
Chicken Shrimp Soup 148
Chicken Teriyaki 63
Chicken Tikka 30
Chicken Yakitori. 78
Chili Dipping Sauce. 121
China
Beefy Spinach Noodles 60
Braised Pork. 94
Chicken And Asparagus. 67
Chicken Noodle Salad 110
Egg Foo Yong 103
Ginger Beef 58
Kung-Pao Chicken 76
Mandarin Pancakes 122
Moo Shu Pork 92
Nutty Steamed Rice. 129
Orange-Flavored Rice. 130
Peppered Chicken 73
Pork And Green Soup 145
Pork Chop Suey. 101
Seafood Dim Sum 91
Stir-Fried Rice. 127
Sweet And Sour Pork 95
Sweet And Sour Sauce. 95
Sweet Corn Chicken Soup 142
Tapioca Pudding 47
Chop Suey, Pork 101
Chutney, Coriander. 37
Chutney, Date. 41

Chutney Sauce 64
Chutney Sauce, Meatballs With. 64
Clams, Rice And 130
Coco-Milk Chicken 70
Coconut
East Indian Coconut Rice 128
Rolled Sole In Coconut Sauce . . . 80
Squash In Coconut Broth. 149
Thai Coconut Rice 131
Coconut Cabbage With Fish 85
Coconut Curry Shrimp 87
Coconut Mango Ice 48
Coconut Sauce 80
Condiments & Spices
Cabbage Kimchee. 33
Coriander Chutney 37
Cucumber Raita. 38
Date Chutney 41
Garam Masala. 40
Indian Chai 40
Indian Side Salad 34
Oi Kimchee 39
Rosy Ginger Pickle 38
Cooked Whole Trout. 81
Coriander Chutney 37
Corn Chicken Soup, Sweet 142
Crab Cakes, Surprise 19
Crisp Fried Brown Onions 133
Crust, Thai Pizza On A Garlic. 66
Cucumber Raita 38
Curry
Chicken Curry Wraps. 74
Coconut Curry Shrimp 87
Dhal 133
Shrimp Mango 86

D

Daikon Carrot Salad 109
Date Chutney 41
Deep-Fried Spring Rolls 28
Desserts & Sweets
Caramel Bananas 46
Coconut Mango Ice. 48
East Indian Ice Cream 42
Gajar Halwa. 45
Kulfi. 42
Strawberry Lassi. 46
Strawberry Snow. 49
Sweet Banana Pudding 44
Sweet Fried Bananas 50
Tapioca Pudding 47
Tapioca With Sweet Cherry 43
Dhal Curry 133
Dim Sum, Seafood 91
Dipping Sauce 117
Dipping Sauces, see Sauces
Double Crunch Salad 105
Dressing, Ginger. 113
Dressing, Thai. 114
Dressing, Vinaigrette 110

E

East Indian Coconut Rice. 128
East Indian Ice Cream 42

153

Egg Foo Yong 103
Eggplant Stir-Fry, Asian 55

F

Fiddlehead Stir-Fry, Pork 97
Fish & Seafood
   Chicken Shrimp Soup 148
   Coconut Cabbage With Fish 85
   Coconut Curry Shrimp 87
   Cooked Whole Trout 81
   Deep-Fried Spring Rolls 28
   Green Onion Pancakes. 15
   Hot And Sour Prawn Soup With
     Lemon Grass 146
   Kujolp'an. 20
   Nasi Goreng 134
   Pad Thai 98
   Pajeon 15
   Pleated Purses 31
   Rice And Clams 130
   Rolled Sole In Coconut Sauce 80
   Sake 88
   Sake Oven. 88
   Sauced Halibut 82
   Seafood Dim Sum 91
   Shrimp Mango Curry. 86
   Somen And Fish 83
   Squash In Coconut Broth. 149
   Surprise Crab Cakes. 19
   Sushi Lettuce Boats 25
   Sushi Stacks. 23
   Tea-Poached Halibut 84
   Tom Yam Goong. 146
Fried Bananas, Sweet. 50
Fried Brown Onions, Crisp. 133
Fried Noodles, Chicken. 68
Fruit
   Caramel Bananas. 46
   Chicken Salad 106
   Coconut Mango Ice. 48
   Great Thai Salad 114
   Minty Pawpaw Salad 116
   Sauced Halibut 82
   Shrimp Mango Curry. 86
   Strawberry Lassi. 46
   Strawberry Snow. 49
   Sweet Banana Pudding 44
   Sweet Fried Bananas 50
   Tapioca Pudding 47
   Tapioca With Sweet Cherry 43

G

Gado-Gado. 111
Gajar Halwa 45
Garam Masala. 40
Garlic Crust, Thai Pizza On A. 66
Ga-Xao-Xa-Ot 65
Ginger
   Honey Ginger Chicken. 77
   Lime Ginger Sauce. 120
   Rosy Ginger Pickle 38
   Two Ginger Sauce 118
Ginger Beef. 58
Ginger Dressing. 113
Great Thai Salad 114
Green Bean Stir-Fry 132

Green Onion Pancakes 15
Grilled Pork, Spicy 99

H

Halibut, Sauced. 82
Halibut, Tea-Poached 84
Honey Ginger Chicken 77
Hot And Sour Prawn Soup With
   Lemon Grass 146
Hot Chicken Crunch 105

I

Ice, Coconut Mango. 48
Ice Cream, East Indian. 42
India
   Chicken Curry Wraps. 74
   Chicken Tikka 30
   Coriander Chutney 37
   Crisp Fried Brown Onions 133
   Cucumber Raita. 38
   Date Chutney 41
   Dhal Curry. 133
   East Indian Coconut Rice 128
   East Indian Ice Cream 42
   Gajar Halwa. 45
   Garam Masala 40
   Indian Chai 40
   Indian Side Salad. 34
   Kulfi. 42
   Pakora. 16
   Potato Raita. 115
   Punjab Chicken 68
   Roti 123
   Saffron Vegetable Pulao. 135
   Sauced Halibut 82
   Strawberry Lassi. 46
   Vegetable Samosas 26
Indian Chai 40
Indian Side Salad. 34
Indonesia
   Coco-Milk Chicken 70
   Cooked Whole Trout 81
   Gado-Gado. 111
   Green Bean Stir-Fry 132
   Nasi Goreng 134

J

Japan
   Beef Teriyaki. 63
   Beef Yakitori 78
   Cabbage Fry 136
   Chicken Shrimp Soup 148
   Chicken Teriyaki. 63
   Chicken Yakitori 78
   Daikon Carrot Salad. 109
   Ginger Dressing. 113
   Japanese Lettuce Salad. 113
   Japanese Omelet 14
   Japanese Primavera 104
   Japan-Style Rice 129
   Miso Dipping Sauce. 117
   Osumashi 147
   Parsley Sushi Rice. 22
   Pink Sushi Rice. 22
   Pork And Peppers 93
   Pork Fiddlehead Stir-Fry 97

Quick Osumashi 147
Rainbow Sushi. 27
Rosy Ginger Pickle 38
Sake Fish 88
Sake Oven Fish 88
Somen And Fish 83
Spiffy Carrots. 136
Spinach Chicken Teriyaki 75
Strawberry Snow. 49
String Beans 132
Sukiyaki 61
Sushi Lettuce Boats 25
Sushi Rice 22
Sushi Stacks. 23
Teriyaki Meatballs 57
Two Ginger Sauce 118
Whirl-A-Gig Sushi. 24
Yellow Sushi Rice 22
Japanese Lettuce Salad 113
Japanese Omelet. 14
Japanese Primavera 104
Japan-Style Rice. 129

K

Kimchee, Cabbage 33
Kimchee, Oi 39
Korea
   Asparagus Sesame 137
   Battered Meatballs. 32
   Bibimbap. 51
   Bulgogi 59
   Cabbage Kimchee 33
   Chap Jae 56
   Dipping Sauce. 117
   Green Onion Pancakes. 15
   Korean Barbecued Beef 59
   Kujolp'an. 20
   Oi Kimchee 39
   Pajeon 15
   Pancake Batter. 20
   Rice And Clams 130
   Spicy Grilled Pork. 99
   Stir-Fry Beef And Noodles 56
   Tender Korean Beef 52
   Veggie Beef Rice Bowl 51
Korean Barbecued Beef 59
Kujolp'an 20
Kulfi 42
Kung-Pao Chicken. 76

L

Lassi, Strawberry 46
Lemon Grass, Hot And Sour Prawn
   Soup With 146
Lemon Grass Pork 100
Lemon Grass, Spicy Chicken With . . . 65
Lettuce Boats, Sushi 25
Lettuce Salad, Japanese 113
Lime Ginger Sauce 120
Lumpia 96

M

Main Courses
   Asian Eggplant Stir-Fry. 55
   Beef Teriyaki. 63
   Beef Yakitori. 78

154

Beefy Spinach Noodles 60
Bibimbap. 51
Braised Pork. 94
Brown Sauce 96
Bulgogi 59
Chap Jae 56
Chicken And Asparagus 67
Chicken And Pork Stew 79
Chicken Curry Wraps 74
Chicken Fried Noodles 68
Chicken Teriyaki. 63
Chicken Yakitori. 78
Coco-Milk Chicken 70
Coconut Cabbage With Fish 85
Coconut Curry Shrimp 87
Cooked Whole Trout 81
Egg Foo Yong 103
Ga-Xao-Xa-Ot 65
Ginger Beef 58
Honey Ginger Chicken. 77
Japanese Primavera 104
Korean Barbecued Beef 59
Kung-Pao Chicken. 76
Lemon Grass Pork 100
Lumpia 96
Meatballs In Tasty Broth 62
Meatballs With Chutney Sauce . . . 64
Moo Shu Pork 92
Pad Thai 98
Peppered Chicken 73
Pork And Peppers 93
Pork Chop Suey 101
Pork Fiddlehead Stir-Fry 97
Punjab Chicken 68
Rolled Sole In Coconut Sauce 80
Sake Fish 88
Sake Oven Fish 88
Sauced Halibut 82
Seafood Dim Sum 91
Shrimp Mango Curry. 86
Somen And Fish 83
Spicy Chicken With Lemon Grass . . 65
Spicy Grilled Pork. 99
Spinach Chicken Teriyaki 75
Stir-Fry Beef And Noodles 56
Sukiyaki 61
Sweet And Sour Pork 95
Sweet And Sour Sauce 95
Tea-Poached Halibut 84
Tender Korean Beef 52
Teriyaki Meatballs 57
Thai Pizza On A Garlic Crust 66
Vegetarian Thai Noodles 102
Veggie Beef Rice Bowl 51
Malaysia
  Chicken Fried Noodles. 68
  Coconut Cabbage With Fish 85
  Malaysian Beef Noodle Soup 141
  Shrimp Mango Curry. 86
  Sweet And Sour Vegetables 138
Malaysian Beef Noodle Soup 141
Mandarin Pancakes 122
Mango Curry, Shrimp 86
Mango Ice, Coconut 48
Masala, Garam 40
Meatballs
  Battered. 32
  Meatballs In Tasty Broth. 62

Meatballs With Chutney Sauce . . . 64
Teriyaki 57
Minty Pawpaw Salad 116
Miso Dipping Sauce 117
Moo Shu Pork 92

N

Nasi Goreng 134
Noodles
  Banh Pho Bo 140
  Beef Noodle Soup 140
  Beefy Spinach 60
  Chap Jae 56
  Chicken Fried. 68
  Chicken Noodle Salad 110
  Deep-Fried Spring Rolls 28
  Japanese Primavera 104
  Lemon Grass Pork 100
  Lumpia 96
  Malaysian Beef Noodle Soup 141
  Pad Thai 98
  Somen And Fish 83
  Stir-Fry Beef And 56
  Sweet Banana Pudding 44
  Vegetarian Thai 102
  Vietnamese Spring Rolls 29
Nuoc Cham 121
Nuoc Leo 120
Nutty Steamed Rice 129

O

Oi Kimchee 39
Omelet, Japanese 14
Onion Pancakes, Green 15
Onions, Crisp Fried Brown 133
Orange-Flavored Rice 130
Osumashi 147
Osumashi, Quick 147
Oven Fish, Sake 88

P

Pad Thai 98
Pajeon 15
Pakora 16
Pancake Batter 20
Pancakes, Green Onion 15
Pancakes, Mandarin 122
Parsley Sushi Rice 22
Pawpaw Salad, Minty 116
Peanut Sauce 119
Peanut Sauce, Vietnamese 120
Peppered Chicken 73
Peppers, Pork And 93
Philippines
  Brown Sauce 96
  Caramel Bananas 46
  Cassava Biscuits 124
  Chicken And Pork Stew 79
  Chicken Salad 106
  Lumpia 96
Pickle, Rosy Ginger 38
Pink Sushi Rice 22
Pizza On A Garlic Crust, Thai 66
Pleated Purses 31
Pork
  Battered Meatballs 32

Braised. 94
Chicken And Pork Stew 79
Deep-Fried Spring Rolls 28
Lemon Grass 100
Lumpia 96
Moo Shu 92
Nasi Goreng 134
Pad Thai 98
Pleated Purses 31
Spicy Grilled 99
Sweet And Sour 95
Sweet Corn Chicken Soup 142
Vietnamese Spring Rolls 29
Pork And Green Soup 145
Pork And Peppers 93
Pork Chop Suey 101
Pork Fiddlehead Stir-Fry 97
Potato Raita 115
Prawn Soup With Lemon Grass,
  Hot And Sour 146
Primavera, Japanese 104
Pudding, Sweet Banana 44
Pudding, Tapioca 47
Pulao, Saffron Vegetable 135
Punjab Chicken 68

Q

Quick Osumashi 147

R

Radish Salad, Spicy 112
Rainbow Sushi 27
Raita, Cucumber 38
Raita, Potato 115
Rice
  Bibimbap. 51
  Chicken Curry Wraps 74
  East Indian Coconut 128
  Japan-Style 129
  Nasi Goreng 134
  Nutty Steamed 129
  Orange-Flavored 130
  Parsley Sushi 22
  Pink Sushi 22
  Rainbow Sushi 27
  Saffron Vegetable Pulao 135
  Stir-Fried 127
  Sushi 22
  Sushi Lettuce Boats 25
  Sushi Stacks 23
  Thai Coconut 131
  Veggie Beef Rice Bowl 51
  Whirl-A-Gig Sushi 24
  Yellow Sushi 22
Rice And Clams 130
Rolled Sole In Coconut Sauce 80
Rosy Ginger Pickle 38
Roti 123

S

Saffron Vegetable Pulao 135
Sake Fish 88
Sake Oven Fish 88
Salads
  Chicken 106
  Chicken Noodle 110

155

Cucumber Raita. 38
Daikon Carrot 109
Double Crunch 105
Gado-Gado 111
Ginger Dressing. 113
Great Thai 114
Hot Chicken Crunch 105
Indian Side 34
Japanese Lettuce 113
Minty Pawpaw 116
Potato Raita. 115
Spicy Radish 112
Thai Dressing. 114
Vinaigrette Dressing. 110
Samosas, Vegetable. 26
Sauced Halibut 82
Sauces
   Brown 96
   Chili Dipping 121
   Chutney 64
   Coconut 80
   Dipping 117
   Lime Ginger. 120
   Miso Dipping. 117
   Nuoc Cham. 121
   Nuoc Leo 120
   Peanut. 119
   Spring Roll Dipping 118
   Sweet And Sour. 95
   Two Ginger 118
   Vietnamese Peanut 120
Seafood Dim Sum. 91
Seafood, see Fish & Seafood
Sesame, Asparagus 137
Shrimp, Coconut Curry. 87
Shrimp Mango Curry 86
Shrimp Soup, Chicken. 148
Sides
   Asparagus Sesame 137
   Cabbage Fry 136
   Cassava Biscuits 124
   Crisp Fried Brown Onions 133
   Dhal Curry. 133
   East Indian Coconut Rice 128
   Green Bean Stir-Fry 132
   Japan-Style Rice 129
   Mandarin Pancakes 122
   Nasi Goreng 134
   Nutty Steamed Rice. 129
   Orange-Flavored Rice. 130
   Rice And Clams 130
   Roti 123
   Saffron Vegetable Pulao 135
   Spiffy Carrots. 136
   Stir-Fried Rice. 127
   Stir-Fry Mixed Vegetables. 139
   String Beans 132
   Sweet And Sour Vegetables 138
   Thai Coconut Rice 131
Sole In Coconut Sauce, Rolled. 80
Somen And Fish 83
Soups
   Banh Pho Bo 140
   Meatballs In Tasty Broth. 62
   Beef Noodle 140

Chicken Shrimp. 148
Hot And Sour Prawn Soup
   With Lemon Grass 146
Malaysian Beef Noodle Soup 141
Osumashi 147
Pork And Green. 145
Quick Osumashi 147
Squash In Coconut Broth. 149
Sweet Corn Chicken 142
Tom Yam Goong. 146
Spicy Chicken With Lemon Grass . . . 65
Spicy Grilled Pork 99
Spicy Radish Salad. 112
Spiffy Carrots 136
Spinach Chicken Teriyaki. 75
Spinach Noodles, Beefy. 60
Spring Roll Dipping Sauce. 118
Spring Rolls, Deep-Fried 28
Spring Rolls, Vietnamese 29
Squash In Coconut Broth 149
Steamed Rice, Nutty 129
Stew, Chicken And Pork 79
Stir-Fried Rice 127
Stir-Fry Beef And Noodles 56
Stir-Fry Mixed Vegetables 139
Strawberry Lassi 46
Strawberry Snow. 49
String Beans 132
Sukiyaki. 61
Surprise Crab Cakes 19
Sushi
   Parsley Sushi Rice. 22
   Pink Sushi Rice. 22
   Rainbow 27
   Whirl-A-Gig 24
   Yellow Sushi Rice 22
Sushi Lettuce Boats 25
Sushi Rice 22
Sushi Stacks. 23
Sweet And Sour Pork. 95
Sweet And Sour Sauce 95
Sweet And Sour Vegetables. 138
Sweet Banana Pudding 44
Sweet Corn Chicken Soup. 142
Sweet Fried Bananas 50

T

Tapioca Pudding 47
Tapioca With Sweet Cherry 43
Tea-Poached Halibut 84
Tender Korean Beef. 52
Teriyaki
   Beef. 63
   Chicken. 63
   Spinach Chicken 75
Teriyaki Meatballs 57
Thai Coconut Rice 131
Thai Dressing 114
Thai Pizza On A Garlic Crust 66
Thailand
   Coconut Curry Shrimp 87
   Coconut Mango Ice. 48
   Great Thai Salad 114
   Hot And Sour Prawn Soup
      With Lemon Grass 146

Lime Ginger Sauce. 120
Minty Pawpaw Salad 116
Pad Thai 98
Peanut Sauce. 119
Pleated Purses 31
Squash In Coconut Broth. 149
Sweet Fried Bananas 50
Tapioca With Sweet Cherry 43
Thai Coconut Rice 131
Thai Dressing. 114
Thai Pizza On A Garlic Crust 66
Tom Yam Goong. 146
Vegetarian Thai Noodles 102
Tom Yam Goong. 146
Trout, Cooked Whole 81
Two Ginger Sauce. 118

V

Vegetable Pulao, Saffron 135
Vegetable Samosas 26
Vegetables
   Green Bean Stir-Fry 132
   Stir-Fry Mixed 139
   String Beans 132
   Sweet And Sour. 138
Vegetarian Thai Noodles 102
Veggie Beef Rice Bowl. 51
Vietnam
   Asian Eggplant Stir-Fry 55
   Banh Pho Bo 140
   Beef Noodle Soup 140
   Chili Dipping Sauce 121
   Coconut Sauce 80
   Deep-Fried Spring Rolls 28
   Ga-Xao-Xa-Ot 65
   Honey Ginger Chicken. 77
   Lemon Grass Pork 100
   Meatballs In Tasty Broth. 62
   Nuoc Cham. 121
   Nuoc Leo 120
   Rolled Sole In Coconut Sauce . . . 80
   Spicy Chicken With Lemon
      Grass 65
   Spring Roll Dipping Sauce 118
   Stir-Fry Mixed Vegetables. 139
   Surprise Crab Cakes. 19
   Sweet Banana Pudding 44
   Tea-Poached Halibut 84
   Vietnamese Peanut Sauce 120
   Vietnamese Spring Rolls 29
Vietnamese Peanut Sauce 120
Vietnamese Spring Rolls. 29
Vinaigrette Dressing 110

W

Whirl-A-Gig Sushi 24
Wraps, Chicken Curry 74

Y

Yakitori, Beef 78
Yakitori, Chicken 78
Yellow Sushi Rice. 22

Feature Recipe from

Cooking for the Seasons

New April 1, 2002

Spring, summer, fall, and winter...each dynamic season boasts spectacular changes in scenery, character, and style. This was the inspiration that led to *Cooking for the Seasons*! Inside you will find more than 240 all-new recipes, carefully selected and beautifully photographed to highlight the best of what each season has to offer for your table.

Asparagus Dip

Celebrate Spring with fresh asparagus in this dip that has just a hint of heat. Serve with crackers and vegetables.

Fresh asparagus, trimmed of tough ends, cut up	3/4 lb.	340 g
Water		
Salad dressing (or mayonnaise)	1/4 cup	60 mL
Sour cream	1/2 cup	125 mL
Chopped fresh dill (or 1/4 tsp., 1 mL, dill weed)	1 tsp.	5 mL
Hot pepper sauce	1 tsp.	5 mL
Onion salt	1/4 tsp.	1 mL
Salt	1/8 tsp.	0.5 mL
Lime Juice	1/2 tsp.	2 mL

Cook asparagus in water in large saucepan until very tender. Drain.

Put remaining 7 ingredients into blender. Add asparagus. Process until smooth. Makes 2 cups (500 mL).

2 tbsp. (30 mL): 35 Calories; 2.9 g Total Fat; 53 mg Sodium; 1 g Protein; 2 g Carbohydrate; trace Dietary Fiber

Company's Coming cookbooks are available at **retail locations** throughout Canada!

See mail order form

Buy any 2 cookbooks—choose a 3rd FREE of equal or less value than the lowest price paid.   *Available in Fren◆

Original Series		CA$14.99 Canada		US$10.99 USA & International	
CODE		**CODE**		**CODE**	
SQ	150 Delicious Squares*	PI	Pies*	ST	Starters*
CA	Casseroles*	LR	Light Recipes*	SF	Stir-Fry*
MU	Muffins & More*	PR	Preserves*	MAM	Make-Ahead Meals*
SA	Salads*	LCA	Light Casseroles*	PB	The Potato Book*
AP	Appetizers	CH	Chicken*	CCLFC	Low-Fat Cooking*
DE	Desserts	KC	Kids Cooking	CCLFP	Low-Fat Pasta*
SS	Soups & Sandwiches	BR	Breads*	AC	Appliance Cooking*
CO	Cookies*	ME	Meatless Cooking*	CFK	Cook For Kids
VE	Vegetables	CT	Cooking For Two*	SCH	Stews, Chilies & Chow◆
MC	Main Courses	BB	Breakfasts & Brunches*	FD	Fondues
PA	Pasta*	SC	Slow Cooker Recipes*	CCBE	The Beef Book
CK	Cakes	PZ	Pizza*	ASI	Asian Cooking
BA	Barbecues*	ODM	One Dish Meals*	CB	The Cheese Book ◀N

May 1/02

Greatest Hits		CA$12.99 Canada		US$9.99 USA & International	
CODE		**CODE**		**CODE**	
BML	Biscuits, Muffins & Loaves*	SAS	Soups & Salads*	ITAL	Italian
DSD	Dips, Spreads & Dressings*	SAW	Sandwiches & Wraps*	MEX	Mexican

Lifestyle Series		CA$16.99 Canada	US$12.99 USA & International
CODE			
GR	Grilling*		
DC	Diabetic Cooking*		

Special Occasion Series		CA$19.99 Canada	US$19.99 USA & International
CODE		**CODE**	
CE	Chocolate Everything*	CFS	Cooking for the Seasons ◀NEW▶
GFK	Gifts from the Kitchen		*April 1/02*

COOKBOOKS

www.**companys**coming.com

visit our ↖web-site

COMPANY'S COMING PUBLISHING LIMITED
2311 - 96 Street
Edmonton, Alberta, Canada T6N 1G3
Tel: (780) 450-6223 Fax: (780) 450-1857

Exclusive Mail
Order Offer
See page 158 for list of cookbooks

Buy **2** Get **1** FREE!
Buy any 2 cookbooks—choose a **3rd FREE**
of equal or less value than the lowest price paid.

Quantity	Code	Title	Price Each	Price Total
			$	$
		don't forget		
		to indicate your		
		free book(s).		
		(see exclusive mail order		
		offer above)		
		please print		

	TOTAL BOOKS (including FREE)	TOTAL BOOKS PURCHASED:	$

	International		Canada & USA	
Plus Shipping & Handling (per destination)	$7.00	(one book)	$5.00	(1-3 books)
Additional Books (including FREE books)	$	($2.00 each)	$	($1.00 each)
Sub-Total	$		$	
Canadian residents add G.S.T(7%)			$	
TOTAL AMOUNT ENCLOSED	$		$	

The Fine Print

- Orders outside Canada must be **PAID IN US FUNDS** by cheque or money order drawn on Canadian or US bank or by credit card.
- Make cheque or money order payable to: **COMPANY'S COMING PUBLISHING LIMITED**.
- Prices are expressed in Canadian dollars for Canada, US dollars for USA & International and are subject to change without prior notice.
- Orders are shipped surface mail. For courier rates, visit our web-site: **www.companyscoming.com** or contact us: **Tel: (780) 450-6223 Fax: (780) 450-1857.**
- Sorry, no C.O.D's.

Gift Giving

- Let us help you with your gift giving!
- We will send cookbooks directly to the recipients of your choice if you give us their names and addresses.
- Please specify the titles you wish to send to each person.
- If you would like to include your personal note or card, we will be pleased to enclose it with your gift order.
- Company's Coming Cookbooks make excellent gifts: Birthdays, bridal showers, Mother's Day, Father's Day, graduation or any occasion...collect them all!

☐ MasterCard.   ☐ VISA

Expiry date

Account #

Name of cardholder

Cardholder's signature

Shipping Address
Send the cookbooks listed above to:

Name:

Street:

City: Prov./State:

Country: Postal Code/Zip:

Tel: (   )

E-mail address:

☐ YES! Please send a catalogue

Please mail or fax to:
Company's Coming Publishing Limited
2311 - 96 Street
Edmonton, Alberta, Canada   T6N 1G3
Fax: (780) 450-1857

Name:_____
Address:_____
_____
e-mail:_____

Reader Survey

We welcome your comments and would love to hear from you.
Please take a few moments to give us your feedback.

1. *Approximately what percentage of the cooking do you do in your home?*_____ %

2. *How many meals do you cook in your home in a typical week?*   _____

3. *How often do you refer to a cookbook (or other source) for recipes?*
- ❏ Everyday
- ❏ A few times a week
- ❏ 2 or 3 times a month
- ❏ Once a month
- ❏ A few times a year
- ❏ Never

4. *What recipe features are most important to you? Rank 1 to 7;*
(1 being most important, 7 being least important).
—— Recipes for everyday cooking
—— Recipes for guests and entertaining
—— Easy recipes; quick to prepare, with everyday ingredients
—— Low-fat or health-conscious recipes
—— Recipes you can trust to work
—— Recipes using exotic ingredients
—— Recipes using fresh ingredients only

5. *What cookbook features are most important to you? Rank 1 to 6;*
(1 being most important, 6 being least important).
—— Lots of color photographs of recipes
—— "How-to" instructions or photos
—— Helpful hints & cooking tips
—— Lay-flat binding (coil or plastic comb)
—— Well organized with complete index
—— Priced low

6. *How many cookbooks have you purchased in the last year?*_____

7. *Of these, how many were gifts?*_____

8. *Age group*
- ❏ Under 18
- ❏ 18 to 24
- ❏ 25 to 34
- ❏ 35 to 44
- ❏ 45 to 54
- ❏ 55 to 64
- ❏ 65+

9. *What do you like best about Company's Coming Cookbooks?*
_____
_____

10. *How could Company's Coming Cookbooks be improved?*
_____
_____

11. *Topics you would like to see published by Company's Coming:*
_____
_____

Thank you for sharing your views. We truly value your input.

ASI